LABOR'S "FORGOTTEN PEOPLE"

The Triumph of Identity Politics

Acknowledgements

Rodney Cavalier, Daryl Melham, Nick Dyrenfurth and Laurie Ferguson provided invaluable background information, and made important comments on various draft chapters. John Robertson, Robert Ray, Joe de Bruyn and Morris Iemma made time to discuss my topic generally and on specific issues, and commented on drafts. Michael Easson made time to discuss my topic generally. Jeremy Sammut read and commented on initial drafts of my manuscript. I was able to discuss various issues on immigration policy with Bob Birrell, who also commented on earlier drafts of chapters. Sandy Rippingale, from the Labor Party's National Secretariat, helped me access important Party documents, particularly relating to the Wyndham Plan and the 1979 Inquiry. My recently departed friend, Jeremy Gilling, helped me in accessing and analysing ABS Labour Force Data.

I am solely responsible for the end product.

Dedication

To my late friend Peter Walsh who left politics with his integrity intact. And to Bill Hayden, who is yet to receive the full credit he deserves for taking charge of rebuilding the parliamentary Labor Party in the wake of the demoralising fall of the Whitlam Government.

Published in 2019 by Connor Court Publishing Pty Ltd

Connor Court Publishing Pty Ltd.

PO Box 7257

Redlands Bay Qld 4165

www.connorcourtpublishing.com.au

sales@connorcourt.com

ISBN: 9781-925826-425

Front cover design: Maria Giordano

Printed and bound in Australia

Foreword

In the conclusion of this important and timely book, Michael Thompson makes what to many will seem a rather implausible claim: that the embrace of identity politics by the ALP – and the Left more generally – poses an "existential threat" to the Party's future.

Thompson's main contention is that the Party has, over recent decades, increasingly distanced itself from the concerns of a large part of its traditional working class base, those he refers to as Labor's "forgotten people", the sort of people who were also called "Howard's battler's" in the wake of the latter's electoral victory in 1996.

This is a section of the electorate that social-democratic parties in Australia and elsewhere have tended to take for granted, a presumption that in the end such people have no alternative than to stick to their traditional loyalties. In these circumstances, especially with manifestly inept political opponents, it might seem safe to indulge the stranger extremities of identity politics (for example the extraordinary emphasis on gender identity in the latest ALP federal platform) and to deprecate, indeed to vilify, some of the concerns of their traditional base, most importantly the impact of large scale immigration.

To the extent such concerns are addressed at all, they are seen in exclusively economic terms, the classical Marxist conceit. What we need is better infrastructure, better planning, more labour market programs, and so on. Get this right and all will fall into place – our base will be happy, we can square the circle.

However there is a growing weight of international evidence that this assumption is just wrong. In their pioneering recent study, the

British scholars Roger Eatwell and Mathew Goodwin analyse the collapse of support for traditional social-democratic parties all over Continental Europe and the corresponding emergence of what they term "national populist" parties that have largely appropriated the old working class base of the centre-left parties.

Parties that barely existed several years ago, such as the AfD (Alternative for Deutschland) in Germany, the Sweden Democrats, as well as the longer-established National Rally led by Marine Le Pen and other similar parties have emerged as major electoral forces. The most recent example of this is the Vox party in Spain, that has surged from miniscule support in the space of a few months to 13 percent in the most recent poll, while in the past year similar parties in Austria and Italy have entered governing coalitions. Collectively they are expected to gain between a quarter and possibly even a third of the vote in European elections scheduled for May 2019. The election of Donald Trump is a further manifestation of this phenomenon, with the loss of states long taken for granted by the Democrats (Pennsylvania, Michigan, Wisconsin) as low-income whites defected in large numbers to Trump.

What has underpinned this shift? Eatwell and Goodwin draw on extensive research to essentially argue that there is much more to it than economic deprivation, and that the dismissal of such parties and their supporters as anti-democratic, indeed neo-fascist, is false. They argue that their popularity is rooted in multiple sources of insecurity brought about by extremely rapid cultural and demographic change, the undermining of national sovereignty and borders, and a profound distrust of political and media elites.

Most importantly, there is a pervasive sense that the concerns of ordinary people are ignored. They cite surveys that show all over Europe very high proportions of the population feel that mainstream politicians are indifferent to the concerns of "people like me".

High on the list of concerns of ordinary people is disquiet about the growing influence of Islam in Europe, especially in light of the huge influx of immigrants triggered by the Syrian civil war in 2015. The Royal Institute of International Affairs (commonly referred to as "Chatham House") conducted a survey in which respondents in 10 European countries, including all the major ones, were asked whether they agreed with the statement: "All further migration from mainly Muslim countries should be stopped".

The results were, in the words of the Chatham House report, "striking and sobering". Across all of the European countries, 55 percent agreed, 25 percent neither agreed nor disagreed, and only 20 percent disagreed. In Britain, for example, 47 percent agreed and 23 percent disagreed. These figures are confirmed by other similar studies.

So what we have is a massive undercurrent of disquiet, largely ignored by the political, media and educational elites. Europe desperately needs an honest debate about Islam, especially the compatibility of its tenets with liberal Western societies, but this has been made extremely difficult by the prospect of accusations of racism or Islamophobia. Such sentiments, especially from the "forgotten people", has been largely driven underground, with the active prosecution of laws against subjectively defined "hate speech".

It is not surprising that with such concerns seen as illegitimate in the mainstream parties – especially parties of the Left – people are starting to turn elsewhere.

What about Australia? Thus far, we have not seen the emergence of parties of similar strength and significance to those described above, certainly not ones able to contemplate participation in governing coalitions.

There are several factors accounting for this. Australia has not, so far, seen the scale of cultural and demographic transformation that has fuelled the growth of populist-nationalist parties in Europe. Furthermore Australia is more genuinely "multicultural" than some European countries, with Muslims, Buddhists and Hindus/Sikhs each constituting roughly two and a half percent of the population.

Another important factor is the nature of our electoral system. The proportional representation systems in a number of European countries such as Germany and Sweden allow an insurgent party to quickly gain a significant parliamentary presence. For example, at the first federal election it ever contested the German AfD secured the election of 94 Bundestag members.

The Australian Senate, elected by proportional representation, does provide one means for parties like Pauline Hanson's One Nation to gain some leverage, but that party has been so rent by division and ineptitude that whatever electoral advantage it manages to achieve is quickly frittered away. The decision by Mark Latham, who led the federal Labor Party in the 2004 election campaign, to join One Nation and run in the NSW elections could well be transformative in this respect.

Clearly these developments do not pose an "existential threat" to the ALP in the short term, but the medium to long term is another matter. The rapidity of the decline of the social-democrats in Europe would have seemed incredible just twenty years ago.

However there is another kind of "existential threat" to the ALP arising from its embrace of identity politics, and for an exemplar of this kind of threat we need to look at what has happened to its sister party in Britain: the risk of the party "losing its soul". The transformation of this once great party of the centre-left into a rancid swamp of anti-Semitism and political extremism is tragic to behold.

This is no longer the party of Clement Attlee and Harold Wilson.

This is a party where those who dissent from the extremist line are subject to threats and intimidation by the activist faction Momentum.

It would be a horrible irony were the ALP to follow this trajectory as a result of the well-intentioned reform proposals designed to open up and democratize the party but which could, as Michael Thompson points out, make it vulnerable to a similar takeover by activist groups like GetUp! as has beset UK Labour.

-- Peter Baldwin, Minister in the Hawke and Keating Governments.

Abbreviations

ABC	Australian Broadcasting Corporation
Accord	Prices and Incomes Accord
ACTU	Australian Council of Trade Unions
AFIC	Australian Federation of Islamic Councils
AIFS	Australian Institute of Family Studies
ALP	Australian Labor Party
AMWU	Australian Manufacturing Workers' Union
AES	Australian Election Study
AYL	Australian Young Labor
BBC	British Broadcasting Corporation
CEPU	Communications Electrical and Plumbing Union
Committee on Migration	2013 Joint Standing Committee on Migration *Inquiry into Migration and Multiculturalism in Australia*
DLP	Democratic Labor Party
ECCV	Ethnic Communities Council of Victoria
Essential Media Report	*Essential Media Report* "Essential Research" (2 August 2016)
FEC	Federal Electorate Council
FPLP	Federal Parliamentary Labor Party
Fitzgerald Report	1989 *Immigration – A commitment to Australia*
ICAC	Independent Commission against Corruption
IHRA	Intersex Human Rights Australia
IWWCV	Islamic Women's Welfare Council of Victoria
LA	NSW Legislative Assembly
LC	NSW Legislative Council
LEAN	Labor Environmental Action Network
LMA	Lebanese Muslim Association
MLA	Member of the Legislative Assembly
Movement	Catholic Social Studies Movement
MSA	Muslim Students Association
NESB	Non-English Speaking Background
NGO	Non-Government Organisation
NOPC	National Organising and Planning Committee

NPF	National Policy Forum
NSW	New South Wales
OECD	Organisation for Economic Co-operation and Development
PD	Italian Democratic Party
Preliminary Islamophobia Report	The University of South Australia's International Centre for Muslim and non-Muslim Understanding Islamophobia, social distance and fear of terrorism in Australia: Preliminary Report
Platform	Labor's National Platform
Rules	ALP National Constitution Rules
SBS	Special Broadcasting Service
SDA	Shop Distributive and Allied Employees Association
SEC	State Electorate Council
SES	Socio-economic status
SPD	German Social Democratic Party
Statement about Immigration	*Essential Media Report* "Statement about immigration" (2016)
Steering Committee	Combined Branches' and Unions' Steering Committee
TAPRI	The Australian Population Research Institute
TWU	Transport Workers Union
UK	United Kingdom
UK Labour	Labour Party (UK)
WA	Western Australia
Wyndham Plan	*Party Re-organisation Recommendations of the General Secretary*
1979 Inquiry	*National Committee of Inquiry: Report and Recommendations to the National Executive March 1979*
1996 Review	*Report by the National Consultative Committee to the ALP National Executive*
2002 Review	*National Committee of Review Report August*
2010 Review	*2010 National Review: Report to the ALP National Executive*
2002 Rules Conference	2002 Special National Rules Conference
2011 Mapping Social Cohesion survey	*Mapping Social Cohesion: The Scanlon Foundation surveys*
2017 Mapping Social Cohesion survey	*Mapping Social Cohesion: The Scanlon Foundation surveys*

Contents

INTRODUCTION

From the early 1970s onwards, the ALP has affected a number of changes to the Party's structure (sometimes referred to as its "organisation") and Labor's policies that have transformed it into a political party that Ben Chifley might well find difficulty relating to.

Indeed, it is argued that the ALP's transformation from a political party with its base in an earlier working class that was committed to improving the economic welfare of ordinary Australians has left Labor vulnerable to being outflanked on its right – due to its "cultural" policies and, motherhood statements in the Party's Platform notwithstanding, to its seeming indifference to the inter-generational poverty, welfare dependency and youth unemployment that is the lot of so many contemporary working class Australians living in Sydney's western and like suburbs in other States and Territories.

The most striking electoral consequence of this transformation to date was the downfall of Paul Keating at the 1996 federal election. Although self-serving, his antagonist at that election, John Howard, in his *Lazarus Rising: A Personal and Political Autobiography* told of the:

> [l]arge swathes of traditional Labor voters [for] the Coalition in 1996, 2001 and 2004. The 'Howard battler' liked the economic security my Government delivered, was *socially conservative*, strongly supported our policy on asylum-seekers and were suspicious of policies which satiated environmental prejudices at the expense of

other people's jobs. He or she felt great pride in the Australian achievement [italics added].[1]

The vote at the 1996 election turned into a rout with Labor losing 13 of its 33 seats in NSW. Equally tellingly, exit polls revealed that the Coalition had won 47 per cent of the blue-collar vote, compared with Labor's 39 per cent.[2]

The ALP's transformation can be seen through the lens of the Party's internal Reviews; the first being established in 1964, the purpose being to deal with perceived flaws in the Party's structure and Labor's policies that were causing internal dissension and electoral grief. First, by examining each of the Reviews' reports, the national and rules conferences that passed resolutions requiring rule changes for the implementation of the Reviews' recommendations. Second, by a detailed analysis of the key issues that arose during the Reviews' deliberations on Party structure and Labor policies: the dominance of unions within the Party, the role of factions, direct member election to the Party's policy making conferences, and Labor's appeal to women, youth and migrants – for notwithstanding the Reviews' recommendations, affirmative action for women is the only policy resolved by the Review process. The analyses will draw on the internal Party debates and public commentary by journalists and academics.

By way of background, the Reviews arose out of the prospect of "Tory" governments federally for two or more terms of office as in 1963, 1977 and 2001 following disastrous election loses, questions as to why Labor lost in 1996, along with Labor's failure to win

---

[1]   John Howard, *Lazarus Rising: A Personal and Political Autobiography* (Pymble, NSW: HarperCollins, 2010), p 485. Of course, they saw his economic policies, particularly *Work Choices,* as a betrayal and they abandoned him.

[2]   John Stone, "Remember, it was Paul Keating," *The Australian Financial Review* 15 March 1996.

government in its own right in 2010. Emotions run high at such times, with frustration, anger and despair rife. Usually at the instigation of the federal parliamentary leader, the Party's highest executive body of the day authorised an assortment of Party secretaries, former and sitting parliamentary elders and senior union officials to undertake what were fairly wide-ranging Reviews, whose stated objective was to "modernise", to "reform" the Party. The message conveyed by each of the Reviews was that, chastened by Labor's electoral fall from grace, the Party is now listening to the people. Each Review, it was said, would make recommendations leading to substantive changes in the Party's structure and Labor's policies, making Labor again fit to govern and, therefore, worthy of the electorate's support.

As to the more significant developments in the Party's structure up until the present, the factions have degenerated into sub-factions and personal fiefdoms that in turn gave rise to a political class that eschews ideology in the pursuit of power. The right and left unions' dominance within the Party came under threat from senior figures on the left who propose increasing the numbers of rank and file members at state conferences, which senior right figures argue would effectively hand control of the Party over to the left. And Labor's days as a "mass" party with a broad membership base and numerous branches may be behind it.

On developments in Labor's policies, the Party is said to have succumbed to identity politics, which has meant, first, threats to freedom of speech by censoring or alleging sexism, racism and the like against anyone questioning campaigns associated with its theories. Second, is the failure to address the serious economic problems confronting Australia today. Hawke and Keating consistently drove major economic reform. Labor has since shown little appetite for tackling such reform; instead, relying on negativity to win office. Third, is the sidelining of working class interests as the focus for Labor's policies. The working class are now Labor's "forgotten people".

Do these developments pose any threat(s) to the ALP's future as a major political force?

The ALP's Machinery

As an understanding of the Party's Rules is crucial for reading about the internal debates and public commentary surrounding the Review's deliberations and recommendations on the Party's structure and Labor's policies, a brief description of those provisions of the Rules follows for those unfamiliar with the Party's machinery. In particular, of the Party's national conference, its national executive, national office bearers, affiliated unions (unions affiliate to state branches), local branches and Party members (most members join their local branch). State and Territories branches have similar structures.

Under the Rules, the national conference is the Party's supreme governing authority. Its decisions are binding on all members and sections (including branches) of the Party. National Conference delegates approve the Party's Platform, elect the national executive, and appoint office-bearers such as the National Secretary (who also serves as National Campaign Director during elections). The national (and special rules) conferences resolve any recommendation from the Party's Reviews that require rule changes for their implementation. National Conference is held triennially, and consists of 400 delegates comprising federal politicians, and delegations from the states and territories, plus three from AYL. There is no requirement under the Rules for affiliated unions to be represented at national conference.

However, state conferences elect their state's delegates to national conference, with 50 per cent of those delegates coming from their state's affiliated unions (although this understates the affiliated unions' actual influence on ballots and decisions taken at state conferences).

The national executive is the chief administrative authority of the Party, subject only to the national conference. Its duties include carrying out national conference decisions; interpreting the national constitution, the Platform and national conference decisions. It can intervene in (and overrule) decisions made by state branches, intervene in preselections and direct members of parliament. It can hear and decide on appeals from any affiliated organisation or Party member. It can also convene conferences and appoint committees. Only national conference can hear appeals from the national executive, and rule on its decisions. The membership of the national executive includes the National President (who is directly elected by the membership, chairs the meetings but who has no voting rights); 20 executive members elected by national conference; and the federal parliamentary leader.

The ALP's policies are to be found in its Platform. However, the Platform only gives policy direction; it does not commit the Party to specific policies. Labor governments should follow the Platform. Having said this, when in government Labor cabinets make decisions in response to changing events, and to set the government's political agenda. The longer a Labor government is in power, the more its cabinet will set the government's agenda[3] – which will involve

---

[3] Shadow Treasurer, Chris Bowen, has suggested that the Platform ties the hands of the parliamentary leader and Caucus by binding them to the then 270 page document. "The time for lengthy, detailed and binding manifesto negotiated through this rather tortured process is well and truly over." As state Labor governments govern without having to go through this process, "it is difficult to see why it still has to be this way federally." Chris Bowen, *Hearts & Minds: A Blueprint for Modern Labor* (Carlton, Vic.: Melbourne University Press, 2013), pp 22-23.

considering advice offered by departmental bureaucracies. The Party's machinery is usually reduced to resolutions endorsing actions taken by the government.[4]

In what follows, the focus will be on the ALP's NSW branch. NSW being the most electorally important state[5] (with 18 of the state's 47 federal seats clustered in outer western Sydney, without capturing virtually all of which Labor does not win office federally[6]); the influence of the NSW right (i.e. centre unity) within the Party; and the two most trenchant critics of the Party's structure being former state and federal politicians from the NSW left; and concern over immigration is arguably most keenly felt in NSW.

---

[4]   Although not invariably, as was demonstrated by the 2008 NSW State Conference's rejection of the Iemma Government's plan to privatise the state's electricity system.

[5]   In its coverage of the 2016 federal election, the ABC commented that, "[w]ith 47 seats, New South Wales MPs make up around a third of the membership of the House of Representatives. This weight of numbers means that NSW is always a critical state to the outcome of a federal election." ABC, Federal Election 2016 Federal Election Preview - NSW.

[6]   This is in part the result of the major re-distribution of electoral boundaries in western Sydney in 1968. And population growth has fed into enrolments at every redistribution since 1968, with the expansion of the House of Representatives to 150 seats and the Senate to 76 seats being legislated by Parliament in 1984 adding further to the electoral importance of western Sydney.

1

THE WHITLAM ERA REVIEWS

This chapter charts the ALP's move from a state based to a federal party, including the role of its first paid, full time federal general secretary, Cyril Stanley Wyndham. Wyndham was the author of the ALP's first internal Review, in which he sought to widen the appeal of Labor beyond a party of the working class. The chapter looks at the fate of Wyndham's recommendations at the 1965 and 1967 Federal Conferences, and how the newly elected federal parliamentary leader, Gough Whitlam, used them in his attempt to shift power from the Party machine to the parliamentary leadership. The chapter goes on to cover the 1979 Inquiry that was established in the wake of Whitlam's crushing defeat as Opposition Leader in 1997, and whose recommendations – following those of Wyndham – sought to downplay Labor's public image as the party of the workers by appealing to supporters of the emerging social movements. It then comments on the Wyndham Plan's recommendations that were put to the 1979 and 1981 National Conferences for resolution.

1964 Wyndham Plan

Cyril Wyndham was well qualified for the position of general secretary, having begun work as a clerk in UK Labour rising to special assistant to Morgan Phillips, the General Secretary. In the 1950s, he and Phillips had argued that policies targeting the middle class would be the key to UK Labour's electoral future. They also believed that to win government, a "mass" party's organisation had to balance centralised power with increased member participation. "It was this belief that Wyndham brought to the leadership of the Labor Party in the 1960s."[7]

In 1957 the federal parliamentary leader of the ALP, Doc Evatt, met Wyndham at the Commonwealth Labour Parties' Conference in London. Evatt was impressed by Wyndham, invited him to come to Australia, and in 1958 recruited him as his press secretary.[8] Wyndham left Evatt's office in 1961 to become Victorian Branch secretary. Then in 1963 he returned to Canberra to take up the position of general secretary.[9] Wyndham remained in this position until his resignation in March 1969. During his years with Evatt and the Victorian Branch, Wyndham had formed the view that branch members were underrepresented at policymaking conferences, and the federal executive lacked power, with the real power residing in dysfunctional state branches. Wyndham later recalled "[t]here was a lot of animosity between the states ... The states ... played one off against the other. ... There was no Australianise. There were six separate states. Federal was notional. In fact it was a bloody nuisance to most of them."[10] Wyndham became an outspoken critic of the Labor Party's structures,

---

[7]   Jo Coghlan and Scott Denton, "Reviewing Labor's Internal Reviews 1966-2010: 'Looking forward, looking backwards'," *Melbourne Journal of Politics* 35 (2012): p 22.
[8]   Stephen Mills, *The Professionals: Strategy, Money and the Rise of the Political Campaigner* (Collingwood, Vic.: Black Inc., 2014), p 54.
[9]   Ibid., p 64.
[10] Ibid., pp 82-83.

attacking those who "indulge in futile exercise of factional strife."[11]

Wyndham played a minor role in the "faceless men" controversy. Under the Party's rules at the time, the federal conference determined Labor policy; the popularly elected parliamentary leaders had no say. Wyndham left the 1963 Federal Conference that the parliamentary leaders were not members of to invite the leader Arthur Calwell and his deputy Gough Whitlam to join the delegates inside, which Calwell refused to do,[12] and so both men were left standing in front of the Kingston Hotel in Canberra where the meeting was being held waiting to be told what policy Labor would fight the upcoming election on.[13] A journalist for *The Daily Telegraph*, Alan Reid, had them photographed; the photo appeared with the caption "36 faceless men" (referring to the 36 members of the federal conference), and was clear evidence of the parliamentary leadership's subservience to the Party machine. Prime Minister Robert Menzies' taunting of Labor with the 36 faceless men was devastating during the 1963 election campaign, and was a major stimulus to the Party's structural reform.

As a parliamentary staffer and Party officer at the time of Evatt's defeat at the 1958 election, and Calwell's narrow defeat in 1961 and disastrous loss in 1963, Wyndham witnessed first-hand the absence of any co-ordinating body to oversee federal election campaigns, with state branches free to run their own campaigns as they saw fit. In the wake of Labor's poor 47.4 per cent primary vote at the 1963 election, at its August 1964 meeting the federal executive resolved that, "the General Secretary be authorised to undertake a thorough

---

[11]   Ibid., p 60.
[12]   Cyril Wyndham, Radio Interview, Late Night Live, Radio National ABC, 7 April 2011, Wyndham was adamant the debacle was Calwell's fault, not the delegates to federal conference.
[13]   The decision they were waiting on was Labor's response to a US request to establish a naval communications base in WA.

and comprehensive review of all aspects of the Party's present federal structure."[14]

Wyndham's plan

A key proposal of Wyndham's Plan was to increase the delegates to, and change the composition of, the federal executive and conference.[15] He recommended the leader and deputy of the parliamentary Labor Party attend the federal executive. He also recommended that the leader and deputy of the parliamentary Labor Party, and the leader and deputy of the Party in the Senate, attend federal conference automatically as delegates with full voting rights.[16] In addition, the parliamentary leader of each state was automatically to be a full delegate.[17] Wyndham proposed reorganising direct representation to federal conference;[18] in particular that affiliated federal trade unions, federal electorate Party organisations, state executives and federal parliamentarians attend as delegates to federal conference.[19] Further, the size of state delegations to federal conference was to be increased from six to ten.[20]

Wyndham wanted to broaden the ALP's appeal to the growing middle class. For him, this entailed changing the perception of the ALP as a union dominated party. Moreover, he wrote dismissively of "[r]eferences to the 'workers', and the 'working class' ... [as]

---

[14]   Federal Executive Report to the 1965 Federal Conference, Paragraph 22 Party Reorganisation, p108.
[15]   Recommendation 9.
[16]   Recommendations 3 and 4. Also, the newly adopted shadow cabinet be afforded ex-officio status with the right to speak but not to vote.
[17]   Recommendation 5.
[18]   Recommendation 7 proposed annual rather than biennial federal conferences and monthly federal executive meetings.
[19]   Recommendation 1.
[20]   Recommendation 2.

just so much meaningless and sometimes offensive jargon in a modern society".[21] Wyndham recommended that the president and secretary of the Federal Labor Women's Organisation attend as full delegates to federal conference.[22] He proposed that a Youth Advisory Committee of six be established to advise the federal conference and the executive.[23] He recommended that state branches and the federal executive develop relationships with professional associations, observing that "[c]oncurrent with the growth of the 'white collar' associations, there has been a falling off in the support of the Party from the industrial unions".[24]

The federal executive's reporting instructions were that Wyndham's findings and recommendations be submitted to a special meeting of the NOPC, who were to make their recommendations and submit them to the next meeting of the federal executive (which was to meet in May 1965); any recommendations of the federal executive were to be forwarded to state branches for their consideration, and the recommendations of the federal executive together with the opinions of the state branches were to be forwarded to the 1965 Federal Conference (which was to meet in August 1965) for its approval or otherwise.

The fate of Wyndham's plan lay in the hands of a left dominated federal conference and executive, and the state branches whose vested interests were in retaining their autonomy as a strong federal organisation would threaten their power within their own states and federally.

---

[21] Cyril Wyndham, "Australian Labor Party Reorganisation: Recommendations of the General Secretary " (1964), p 19.

[22] Recommendation 6.

[23] Recommendation 21.

[24] Wyndham, "Australian Labor Party Reorganisation: Recommendations of the General Secretary " p 19.

1965 Federal Conference

Wyndham's Plan was debated at the 1965 Federal Conference, which resolved to take no action on his recommendations. It came as no surprise to Wyndham when the federal conference's and executive's responses were "lukewarm".[25] Wyndham said he always believed his recommendations would not get much support, as they sought to transfer power from the Party's state leaders who enjoyed it to Labor's branch members who had none.[26]

Whitlam's use of Wyndham's recommendations

In his address to the 1965 Federal Conference, Whitlam told delegates that:

> Mr Wyndham symbolises the fact that the Labor Party is now becoming a national Party instead of a collection of six state parties. … His proposals for Federal reorganisation of the Party would give the rank and file of the Party and its affiliates the same degree of participation in Federal decisions and organisation as they already have in State decisions and organisation. They would give Parliamentarians the same direct participation in the affairs of the Australian Labor Party as they have in all socialist parties.[27]

Whitlam was to campaign in support of Wyndham's recommendations,[28] using the call for wide ranging reform to challenge Calwell for the parliamentary leadership and the authority of the "12 witless men" (as he called the 12 members

---

[25] Declan O'Connell, "Party Reform: Debates & Dilemmas, 1958-1991," in *A Century of Social Change: Labor History Essays, Volume 4*, ed. Australian Labor Party. New South Wales Branch (Leichhardt, N.S.W: Pluto Press Australia, 1992), p 141.

[26] Cyril Wyndham, Radio National ABC Interview, Late Night Live, 7 April 2011.

[27] Gough Whitlam, "Address to the ALP Federal Conference," (4 August 1965).

[28] Mills, *The Professionals: Strategy, Money and the Rise of the Political Campaigner*, p 62.

of the federal executive[29]), appealing directly to members so as to pressure federal conference. "[Whitlam] put the prestige of a new leader on the line, taking every opportunity to address branch meetings, union meetings and conferences on the idea of reform." [30] He used Wyndham's recommendations as a means of consolidating federal power in the hands of the parliamentary leadership, particularly their direct representation at federal conference and on the federal executive. Branch member representation was ultimately a lesser priority for him. "Yet it was through the appeal of the idea of rank-and-file representation that Whitlam was able to achieve so much". [31]

1967 Federal Conference

The 1967 Federal Conference resolved that the federal parliamentary leader and deputy, and the Senate leader and deputy, would be members *ex officio* of the federal executive, and that the four federal parliamentary leaders and the six state parliamentary leaders would be delegates *ex officio* to the federal conference. Although short of the reforms he had campaigned for, and admitting further reforms were needed, Whitlam nonetheless claimed the reforms were "the greatest change in the framework of our Party on a national scale since the formation of the federal executive in 1915."[32] Whitlam was

---

[29] Don. Whitington, *The Witless Men* (Melbourne: Sun Books, 1975)., The federal executive had frequently challenged Whitlam's authority. Referring to the federal executive in February of 1966, Whitlam remarked that "I can only say we've got rid of the 36 Faceless Men Stigma to be faced with the twelve witless men".

[30] Graham Freudenberg, *A Certain Grandeur: Gough Whitlam's Life in Politics* (South Melbourne, Vic.: Sun Books, 1978), pp 91-2.

[31] Ibid., p 91.

[32] Ross McMullin, *The Light on the Hill: The Australian Labor Party, 1891-1991* (Oxford: Oxford University Press Australia, 1991), p 318.

sure Labor had "demolished the cry of the 36 faceless men."[33]

1979 Inquiry

The 1979 Inquiry was established by the national executive in January of 1978, following the disastrous December 1977 election defeat. The ALP's primary vote at that election slumped to 39.6 per cent, its lowest since 1949, losing ground on its 1975 result of 42.8 per cent.[34]

The motion establishing the 1979 Inquiry was moved by the federal parliamentary leader, Bill Hayden, who was to be joint chairman along with Bob Hawke, then President of the ACTU.

Hayden had been appointed Minister for Social Security following Whitlam's victory at the 1972 election; he went on to replace Jim Cairns as Treasurer in 1975, serving for five months before the Whitlam Government was dismissed. Hayden challenged Whitlam for the parliamentary leadership early in 1977, and although narrowly defeated he succeeded Whitlam as Opposition Leader following Labor's demoralising defeat at the 1977 election.[35]

Hayden had inherited a Party in crisis. As he later recalled, "Morale was on the floor, people were milling about in a confused state. That three years had to be a period of regrouping, consolidation and trying to lift the morale of the troops."[36] But what drove the 1979 Inquiry was working out how to win the next election. Sol Excel, a member and leading author of the 1979 Inquiry's report, wrote years later that

---

[33] Ibid.

[34] Gerard Newman, "Federal Election Results 1949-1998," *Research Paper* (1999).

[35] Hayden led the Party at the 1980 election, but while recording a substantial swing to Labor, failed to win government. He was deposed by Bob Hawke a few weeks before the 1983 federal election, after months of media speculation.

[36] Bill Hayden, *Sydney Morning Herald*, 27 January 1981.

the main concern of the 1979 Inquiry was the need to project an image of the ALP that voters could identify with, and would respond to.[37]

The 1979 Inquiry held eight meetings, many sub-committee meetings, and received 320 written submissions. It noted that its meetings and submissions revealed a desire for a more "democratic national Party" organisation, for a "reconsideration" of the links between the Party and the trade union movement (concern was expressed at the Coalition's use of the Party's formal links to the unions), and "for greater attention to *neglected elements* of the population – rural voters, white collar workers, women, youth and migrants [italics added]".[38] There were also calls for a greater involvement by the Party with local community groups.

Echoing Wyndham, the 1979 Inquiry found that the Party's organisation and policy making needed to respond to the "rapidly changing society",[39] and that this accounted for the attention paid by it to the changes in gender roles, ethnic diversity and social class identification taking place in Australian society at the time. The 1979 Inquiry called on the Party to do more to appeal to white collar workers, women, ethnic communities and young voters.[40]

The 1979 Inquiry recommended the ALP adopt a policy of affirmative action in favour of women, including that they be guaranteed representation at Party conferences and on Party

---

[37]   Sol Encel, "Labor and the Future: Where to now?," *Evatt Journal* 5, no. 2.
[38]   Bill. Hayden and Bob. Hawke, "National Committee of Inquiry," (Australian Labor Party, 1979), p 3.
[39]   Ibid., p 1.
[40]   Michael Thompson, *Labor without class: The gentrification of the ALP* (Annandale, NSW: Pluto Press in association with the Lloyd Ross Forum, Labour Council of New South Wales, 1999), pp 16-19.

executives.[41] It noted the relative weakness of female support for the ALP, believing the reasons for this were complex, but highlighting the greater conservatism of women voters. In the long run, however, it argued that the move by women from a "predominantly domestic role" to the full-time paid workforce was likely to reduce the difference between male and female voters. For the immediate future (a fixed period of seven or ten years), affirmative action (i.e. quotas) was imperative, if only for "electoral purposes".[42] Sol Encel claimed that "[a]ffirmative action for women dates effectively from this report".[43]

The 1979 Inquiry recommended that two delegates be elected to Party conference by AYL.[44] It also made a series of recommendations regarding ethnic communities, including establishing community branches, conducting meetings in a language other than English, and setting up groups of ethnic ALP members at appropriate levels to act as liaison between the Party and their communities (informal links with ethnic leaders already existed).[45]

Of the reforms to the Party's structure that the 1979 Inquiry recommended, arguably the most important and contentious was a national conference comprising 310 delegates, with direct election of delegates from federal electorate organisations and federal trade unions.

---

[41] Recommendation G1

[42] Recommendation G1

[43] Encel, "Labor and the Future: Where to now?."

[44] Recommendation L1(e)

[45] Rodney Cavalier, *Power Crisis: The Self-destruction of a State Labor Party* (Port Melbourne, Vic.: Cambridge University Press, 2010), pp 48-49. Cavalier claimed that all these proposals have been tried by different state and local branches, but none have reversed the collapse in Party membership.

1979 and 1981 National Conferences

The 1979 Inquiry suggested that its recommendations for reform of national conference be placed on the agenda for discussion at the 1979 National Conference, with a view to their ultimate resolution at the 1981 National Conference. The latter Conference established a national conference of 100 delegates comprising the four federal parliamentary leaders, state and territory delegations comprising a base component of six from each state, plus a supplementary component proportional to the number of House of Representative seats, with at least 25 per cent of each delegation to be women, and one delegate from AYL.

2

REVIEWS CONDUCTED FOLLOWING KEATING'S DEFEAT

This chapter covers the Reviews conducted following Paul Keating's defeat in 1996 and John Howard's victory in 2001, which led to the establishment of the 1996 and 2002 Reviews, respectively. The1996 Review was primarily concerned with the lessons to be learned from Prime Minister Paul Keating's ignoring head office input and running his own election campaign – with disastrous results. Factionalism was also raised by the 1996 Review, but it made no recommendations to deal with it. Indeed, it chose not to propose large scale structural changes. While supporting the affirmative action quota for women of 35 per cent, the 1996 Review rebuked those who failed to understand the difficulty of implementing the policy. The 2002 Review saw the major issue facing Labor as its declining primary vote – in particular Labor had failed to retain the support of blue collar workers and women from low socio-economic backgrounds, and Labor's candidates needed to represent the broad range of opinion and experience of the nation. The 2002 Review found no evidence of the unions being a liability at the 2002 election. Its consultations revealed the major issues for its supporters were affirmative action for women and factionalism. The 2002 Review recommended a target for affirmative action for women of 35 per cent, reduced union representation at state conferences and measures to deal with branch stacking. The Party's 2002 Rules Conference resolved to raise the affirmative action for women quota from 35 per cent to 40 per cent and reduce the proportion of union delegates to state conference.

1996 Review

The 1996 Review was requested by the National Executive, the objective being to develop "Labor's organisational agenda for the future". In contrast to earlier, and most subsequent, internal Reviews, the 1996 Review focused on what had gone wrong in the re-election campaign of a Labor (Keating) Government that had been toppled, and where its primary vote had fallen to just 38.8 per cent.[46]

Stephen Mills explained what led the Party to establish the 1996 Review: "Prime Minister Paul Keating ... rejected ... the authority of the national campaign director and shook off the centralised discipline of ... head office. [Keating] tried to direct [his] own campaign strategy ... [which] led to humiliating electoral defeat."[47] For all professionals within the Labor Party, "this campaign has become a template for how not to run an election campaign".[48]

The 1996 Review met in all state capitals, and spoke with Party members and members of state branch administrative committees. It also received submissions via the ALP's home page.

---

[46] *Detailed results: House of Representatives 1990-2013*, aph.gov.au.
[47] Mills, *The Professionals: Strategy, Money and the Rise of the Political Campaigner*, p 157.
[48] Ibid.

The review of a failed election campaign

The 1996 Review focused on the political action that it was necessary to take now,[49] with its recommendations almost exclusively concerned with communications and campaigning. The recommendations dealing with communication called for action by the national secretary on electoral education seminars;[50] a free call information system;[51] and, in consultation with state branches, extending the ALP's Home Page information system to state branches.[52]

However, most of the 1996 Review's recommendations dealt with campaigning. Specifically, that the national secretariat provide a new campaign manual,[53] and a campaign update bulletin for local branch secretaries (following national executive meetings);[54] that the national secretariat continue to liaise with state offices on the production of regular mail outs of campaign notes; that it develop a history of Labor and biography documents for dissemination via booklets, internet and the *National Herald*;[55] that the *National Herald* be adopted by all state and territory branches (and it include a "Campaign Active" supplement to assist with local campaigns);[56] that the national secretary, in consultation with state branch secretaries, produce campaign materials suitable for regional Australia,[57] and institute a system of campaign auditing to

---

[49] National Consultative Review Committee, "Report by the National Consultative Review Committee to the ALP National Executive," (ALP, August 1996), p 2.

[50] Recommendation 1.2

[51] Recommendation 1.5

[52] Recommendation 1.6

[53] Recommendation 1.1

[54] Recommendation 1.3

[55] Recommendation 1.3

[56] Recommendation 1.3

[57] Recommendation 1.4

include central campaign structures;[58] and that the Party "continually monitor changes in campaign technology and ideas to ensure that our tactics are always up to date".[59] It stated that campaign ideas are important, and to "ensure that our campaigning remains state of the art we must be alert".[60] It recommended the national secretary ensure that overseas visitor programs are biased towards participants who can obtain campaigning experience (including developing Labor's position at the Socialist International) to "emphasise the gathering and exchange of ideas from international campaigns".[61] The 1996 Review's recommendations did not require any rule changes.

Factionalism

The 1996 Review stated that it was not its intention to "prescribe massive organisational changes".[62] And although it did discuss factionalism, it made no recommendation(s). The 1996 Review argued that the formalisation of factions was a "very useful management tool", providing a means of consultation, avoiding and resolving disputes over policies, and filling positions. But it acknowledged that, rightly or wrongly, factions are seen "publicly and within the Party" as a major problem, and they "occasionally become an end in themselves, a recruitment agency and a patronage system". The report stated that "winning preselection as the result of endorsement by factional leaders alone weakens candidates electorally".[63]

---

58 Recommendation 3.1
59 Recommendation 3.3
60 Recommendation 3.2
61 Recommendation 3.2
62 National Consultative Review Committee, "Report by the National Consultative Review Committee to the ALP National Executive," p 2.
63 Ibid., p 5.

Affirmative action for women

The 1996 Review's report to the national executive was to include an examination of the arrangements each state branch had in place to ensure the Party's commitment to affirmative action was progressively implemented during the next round of federal preselections.[64] It affirmed the "commitment to achieve the 35 per cent target by 2002", and state branches were to "implement candidate and activist training programs" to assist in the development of candidates and, therefore, achievement of the target. It reported that "Party members expressed opposing views".[65] Many women thought the 35 per cent quota by 2002 was "condescending", while others aggressively argued for it.[66] The 1996 Review was critical of the many who argued against the Party on this issue, as they were "the very people who should have acknowledged the care and difficulty required in making affirmative action work".[67]

2002 Review

Following the 2001 federal election rout,[68] at which only 37.8 per cent of first preference votes went to Labor,[69] lower than at any of its demoralising loses in 1975, 1977 and 1996, and its lowest primary vote since 1906, Labor's newly elected federal parliamentary leader, Simon Crean, announced a review of the Party's organisation, structure and internal processes. To undertake it, the National Executive resolved

---

[64] Ibid. Appendix
[65] Ibid., p 7.
[66] Ibid.
[67] Ibid.
[68] Neville Wran put the loss down to the *Tampa* incident, as did Bob Hawke, who thought 9/11 was also a contributing factor. Simon Crean et al., interview by Louise. Yaxley, 9 August, 2002.
[69] Detailed results: House of Representatives 1990-2013, www.aph.gov.au

at its meeting on the 31 December 2001 to establish the 2002 Review, to be conducted by two of the Labor Party's most successful former leaders, Prime Minister Bob Hawke and NSW Premier Neville Wran

The 2002 Review consulted extensively with Party members and interested groups, and it received 669 written submissions.

The 2002 Review was asked to examine and report on preselection and policy development processes, the ALP's relationships with the unions and community groups, strategies to increase Labor's primary vote at federal elections, measures to increase Party membership, and the Party's internal processes.[70] John Button thought the 2002 Review's terms of reference were similar to those of the 1979 Inquiry, on which Button was Bill Hayden's proxy,[71] suggesting that few substantive changes had been made since 1979.

The "challenge" of a declining primary vote

The 2002 Review saw the decline in Labor's primary vote as the "challenge" facing the Party, as it had increased Labor's dependency on second preferences from the minor parties. This dependence was "partly attributable to the decline in 'Party identification' experienced in comparable democracies elsewhere".[72] In Australia, this meant the "major political parties can no longer rely on a large base of loyal electors: support must be gained and carefully maintained, and no one can be taken for granted".[73] In particular, it reported that Labor had failed to retain the support of skilled and semi-skilled blue collar workers and women from lower socio-economic backgrounds. The

---

[70] Bob Hawke and Neville Wran, "National Committee of Review," (2002), p 6.
[71] John Button, "Beyond Belief: What Future for Labor?," *Quarterly Essay* no. 6 (2002): p 48.
[72] Hawke and Wran, "National Committee of Review," p 9.
[73] Ibid.

2002 Review argued that the Party needed to present a diverse group of candidates to the electorate, one that represents the broad range of opinions and experiences in the Party and in the nation as a whole.

The rebuilding of Labor's voter base, the 2002 Review argued, had to begin with a thorough restatement of the Party's values (it proposed that the Party develop a statement conveying "modern Labor's objectives and aspirations" that can be communicated to members and the Australian community), and the most appropriate ways of transforming them into policy.[74]

Themes from the consultations

Of the "themes" that emerged from the 2002 Review's consultations, the clearest was the level and nature of factionalism in the Party, "and the detrimental effect this has on internal democratic processes".[75] The report noted that many members viewed "National Conference as a stage-managed affair run by factional leaders, devoid of real policy debate, and inaccessible to the rank and file". In the view of many submissions, the "factions now hold too central and too strong a grip on policy and candidate selection". The factions were associated with the third most raised theme of branch stacking, and "the cancerous effect this activity has on the democratic traditions that have been the strength of our Party".[76]

Other themes raised in a significant number of submissions included "Affirmative Action and the need to continue to increase women's participation at all levels",[77] and the "dwindling" branch

---

[74]   Ibid., p 9.
[75]   Ibid., p 8.
[76]   Ibid.
[77]   Ibid.

membership. "All agreed Labor must act to gain the long-term support of new voters, cement the backing of swinging voters and prevent previously loyal ALP voters drifting away to the other parties."[78] Some submissions suggested Labor had lost touch with its traditional blue-collar base, others that not enough was done to win the support of "aspirational" voters, "however defined".

The 2002 Review reported that many rank and file trade unionists and their national officials expressed concern that some in the Party had sought, "at least by inference", to shift blame for the loss in 2001 onto the union movement. However, the 2002 Review found no evidence to support the claim that unions were a liability for Labor at the 2001 election.[79]

Recommendations

The 2002 Review set out "principles" for the structure of future national conferences.[80] The major focus of which – and its most contentious principle – was a rule to reduce union representation at state conferences from a ratio of 60:40[81] to 50:50,[82] so as to reflect the "equal partnership"[83] between the Party and the union movement. The principles also included significantly increasing the size of national conference, with participation of rank and file members to be "encouraged" through the direct election of a component of such delegates.

---

[78] Ibid., p 9.

[79] Ibid., p 17.

[80] Recommendations 1 and 17.

[81] Hawke and Wran, "National Committee of Review," p 19.

[82] Also, 18 and 19 recommended that union delegations to state conferences only comprise members of that particular union, and that union affiliation to the Party be determined by a 'snapshot' audit of members at periodic intervals.

[83] The term equal partnership appears in Recommendations 1 and 17 of the 2002 Review's report.

As for factionalism, "[i]t was not the intention of the review to recommend any changes".[84]

The 2002 Review discussed branch stacking in detail,[85] and proposed important measures to "further strengthen efforts to control 'branch stacking'" (which it defined as "when membership lists are artificially inflated with large numbers of 'members' lacking commitment to the Party").[86] Those measures included:

- prohibiting "bulk renewals" (i.e. where memberships are renewed en masse by a third party);

- introducing a standard renewal form, requiring an individual's signature authorising their renewal;

- consideration be given to strengthening state rules limiting the number of people who can join a local branch at any one time;

- permitting members to petition a state executive or administrative committee to investigate branch stacking in a federal seat;

- the national executive continue its role in monitoring branch stacking (and other forms of membership manipulation); and

- the establishment of a national appeals tribunal to "ensure the Party provides proper appeals mechanisms for members", such as when a member believes the new anti-branch stacking rules are not being followed.

The 2002 Review further recommended the establishment of different forms of branches, such as policy branches; on-line branches; branches on university and TAFE campuses; occupation, workplace and employment branches. It recommended branches in

---

[84]   Crean et al., "Crean to fight for Hawke-Wran proposals."
[85]   Hawke and Wran, "National Committee of Review," pp 13-15.Recommendations 9, 10 and 11.
[86]   Ibid., p 13.

metropolitan areas be consolidated. It proposed that Labor "explore the possibility of the creation of an associate class of membership as a way of broadening involvement in the Party", and that the federal ALP consult with, among others, welfare and community groups.[87]

The 2002 Review also recommended that a rule be developed with a target of "no less than 35 per cent" for women (the existing quota) that would provide a new deadline and an enforcement mechanism, "if necessary", by the national executive.[88]

The 2002 Review proposed that its recommendations requiring rule changes – branch stacking, a national appeals tribunal, union representation at state conferences and affirmative action for women – be referred to the Rules Conference that was announced by Crean in July 2002, and was to be held in October of that year. Its other recommendations – those dealing with different forms of branches, candidates for preselections, associate membership and its relationships with third parties – were set out in its report to the National Executive.

2002 Rules Conference

The 2002 Rules Conference passed a resolution calling for a reduction in union representation at the Party's state conferences from 60: 40 to 50: 50. Other resolutions passed included those dealing with branch stacking, a national appeals tribunal and affirmative action for women – raising the quota of winnable seats for women

---

[87]   Recommendation 21.

[88]   30 and 31, recommended requiring state branches to provide annual affirmative action reports to their executives and national executive on the "implementation of Affirmative Action measures at both the organisational and parliamentary levels", and that the role of the Labor Women's Network be made clear in the national rules.

from 35 to 40 per cent, but with the compliance date pushed back to 2012. Although not a recommendation referred to it by the 2002 Review, the 2002 Rules Conference passed a resolution for rank and file member preselection of the national president. But a resolution to directly elect member delegates to national conference failed.

3

THE RUDD/GILLARD REVIEW

The most recent Review was conducted in 2010. It was noteworthy for two of its three sections being withheld from the public (although they were effectively made public by being leaked to the media). It painted a depressing picture of a collapse in, and ageing of, Party membership (instancing NSW); it made minor recommendations for reforming the Party's structure aimed at increasing membership, including targeting voters lost to the Greens and conducting research on voters attracted to the Greens (no such recommendations were made for Labor supporters lost to parties on the right). It commented that branch stacking had largely been curtailed. The 2010 Review's two "secret" sections made recommendations aimed at ensuring there would be no repeat of certain aspects of the Rudd Government's performance, nor of the Gillard Government's 2010 election campaign. The 2011 National Conference passed resolutions for minor reforms to the Party's structure, including an increase in directly elected members to national conference. The 2015 National Conference increased to 150 the members directly election to national conference and to 50 per cent by 2025 the affirmative action quota for women, but it rejected reform of Senate pre-selections.

As for the parliamentary leadership merry-go-round leading up to and during the Rudd Gillard years, following Labor's defeat in the 1996 election the Deputy Prime Minister Kim Beazley was elected unopposed as Labor's parliamentary leader, replacing Paul Keating. Beazley led Labor at the 1998 election, where it polled a majority of the two-party vote but fell eight seats short of winning government. After leading Labor to a second defeat at the 2001 election, Beazley resigned the parliamentary leadership in favour of his deputy Simon Crean. But then in 2003 Beazley made two attempts to regain the parliamentary leadership. He lost a challenge to Crean in June and, following Crean's resignation as parliamentary leader, Beazley lost a ballot to Shadow Cabinet Minister Mark Latham in December by just two votes. However, Beazley was elected parliamentary leader a second time in 2005, after Latham's resignation in the wake of Labor's 2004 election defeat, only to be replaced by the Shadow Minister for Foreign Affairs Kevin Rudd in 2006, following a series of poor opinion poll results. With the retirement of Beazley at the 2007 election, the younger generation of leaders had finally entrenched themselves. Rudd was replaced as Prime Minister by Julia Gillard (the justification for this was extensively commented on in the 2010 Review). However, polling in early June 2013 suggested that Labor could be left with only 40 seats in federal parliament. On 26 June 2013, Julia Gillard called a leadership spill. Rudd announced he would challenge the Prime Minister. Bill Shorten, a key Gillard supporter, who was one of the main figures behind Rudd's downfall as Prime Minister, this time round supported Rudd. Rudd subsequently won the leadership ballot, 57–45, and became the parliamentary leader and Prime Minister for the second time.

2010 Review

The 2010 Review was established at the request of Prime Minister Julia Gillard, following the formation of her minority government, Labor having gained only 38 per cent of the primary vote at the 2010 election.[89] To conduct it, the National Executive commissioned former Victorian Premier Steve Bracks, former NSW Premier Bob Carr and NSW Senator John Faulkner (a senior minister in the two governments under examination by the 2010 Review).The 2010 Review received 800 written submissions, and over 3,500 via its website.[90]

The "crisis in membership"

The 2010 Review reported that the Party was facing a "crisis in membership".[91] Evidence of this decline could no longer be ignored. In NSW alone, more than 100 branches had closed in the last decade, and the Party's national membership, standing at 45,000, represented only 0.0002 per cent of the Australian population. "Today, the Labor Party struggles to staff polling booths, even in held seats."[92] Members feeling "alienated and disenfranchised" was caused, in large part, by modern campaigning techniques that "diminished and degraded" the role once played by members in political campaigns.[93] But Labor's decline in membership, it argued, also reflected social changes taking place in Western European states, where social democratic parties' support base had been "devoured by Green or left-leaning parties on the one hand and right wing populist parties with a largely anti-

---

[89] *Detailed results: House of Representatives 1990-2013*, aph.gov.au.
[90] ALP, "2010 ALP National Review Report," news release, 2010.
[91] Steve Bracks, John Faulkner, and Bob Carr, "2010 National Review: Report to the ALP National Executive," (Australian Labor Party, 2010), p 9.
[92] Ibid., p 12.
[93] Ibid., p 11.

immigrant agenda, on the other".[94]

Labor's ageing membership was also highlighted. The authors claimed that, "[t]hroughout the Review process and in every part of Australia, the Review Committee was continually reminded by members that the membership of the Party is ageing. As existing members retire from active membership in coming years, the decline will become even more severe."[95]

The three sections of the 2010 Review's report

The 2010 Review was conducted in secret. Its report was published in three sections: the first focused on Kevin Rudd's Government; the second, Labor's 2010 federal election campaign under Julia Gillard's leadership; the third dealt with the Party's structure – "with the future of the Labor Party and the changes that [the authors] believe must occur for the Party to survive and prosper".[96] Only this last section of the 2010 Review's report was released to the public, whereas all previous Reviews' full reports had been publicly released. The secrecy surrounding the 2010 Review occurred notwithstanding that the full report was initially intended to be made public.[97] It was conducted for the benefit of Party members, with "a number of recommendations … directly drawn from the consultative process" with members and supporters,[98] Bracks, Faulkner and Carr all called for it to be released, as did Rudd, despite its criticisms of his government.[99] Troy Bramston

---

[94]   Ibid.

[95]   Ibid., p 10.

[96]   Ibid., p 5.

[97]   Troy Bramston, *Looking for the Light on the Hill: Modern Labor's Challenges* (Carlton North, Vic.: Scribe, 2011), p 205.

[98]   Bracks, Faulkner, and Carr, "2010 National Review: Report to the ALP National Executive," p 6.

[99]   Matthew Franklin and Milanda Rout, "ALP Review authors urge no more secrets," *The Australian*, 6 December 2011.

reported that the withholding of the full report was the decision of Prime Minister Gillard's Office, the national executive and the Party headquarters.[100]

The third section's terms of reference

The terms of reference for the publicly released third section included the need to:[101]

- broaden participation in the Party to ensure a greater say for members, supporters and "stakeholders"; and
- improve dialogue and engagement between "progressive" Australians and the Party, including "progressive" third party organisations.[102]

The "fundamental challenge facing the modern Labor Party"

The 2010 Review's publicly released section argued that "developing a modern and meaningful role for members within a democratic party is the fundamental challenge facing the modern Labor Party".[103] It recommended structural reforms to meet this challenge, and thereby redress the Party's falling membership. They included re-engaging with members by conducting a national survey seeking their views on the Party, and suggestions on improving its structure;[104] growing membership by setting a target;[105] [106] giving members a direct vote for national conference delegates;[107] giving

---

[100] Troy Bramston, "Powerbrokers give elders the brush," ibid.
[101] It is unusual for a terms of reference to dictate conclusions/recommendations.
[102] Bracks, Faulkner, and Carr, "2010 National Review: Report to the ALP National Executive," p 5.
[103] Ibid., p 12.
[104] Recommendation 2.
[105] Recommendations 3 and 4.
[106] Recommendation 8.
[107] Recommendation 11.

members a "strong advocate" by making the national president a voting member of the national executive;[108] encouraging community engagement by introducing primaries for preselections in non-held and open seats;[109] ensuring interventions by the national executive and state administrative committees only occur as a last resort, and then only in exceptional circumstances;[110] and creating an outreach organisation via an on-line presence for engaging with "progressive" Australians and promoting "progressive" campaigns.[111] The 2010 Review commented that, for Labor to effectively develop and articulate a modern reform agenda, it must stay closely connected to the "progressive" movements.

The 2010 Review noted evidence from state and territory Party officials that, while the practice of branch stacking had largely been "curtailed" by the reforms of the late 1990s and 2000s, a new practice of "branch stripping" has arisen in its place, which involves discouraging branches from recruiting members that "allows individuals to then exert greater influence over the outcome of ballots and contests for positions".[112] However, the 2010 Review argued that the only way to confront these practices is to "open up the processes of the Party to greater involvement by the members themselves, thus giving them the responsibility of deciding who will represent them at the highest levels of the Party".[113]

---

[108] Recommendation 13.
[109] Recommendation 26.
[110] Recommendation 25.
[111] Recommendation 27
[112] Bracks, Faulkner, and Carr, "2010 National Review: Report to the ALP National Executive," pp 17-18.
[113] Ibid., p 18.

The first and second "secret" sections

Other than the 1996 Review, the 2010 Review was noteworthy for being the only Review to examine the Party's running of a federal election campaign – the 35 day campaign in 2010 under Julia Gillard's leadership, and the only one to examine the political strategy and tactics of Labor in office – the Rudd's Government.

A Troy Bramston "exclusive" in *The Australian* revealed the 2010 Review had found that the Rudd Government was characterised by "centralised decision making, poor communication, policy backflips and a short-term focus".[114] The authors of the report left the distinct impression that "Ms Gillard's decision to challenge Mr Rudd for the Party leadership, and consequently the prime ministership, was justified".[115] An "apparent chaos at the heart of the government" and a series of "policy errors" [116] precipitated Caucus's recognition that a leadership change was needed, once Gillard had signalled her intention to challenge for the leadership.[117]

The first section's review of the Rudd Government's performance led to 21 recommendations, including the following:

- The December 2011 National Conference should resolve whether the Party leader should possess sole authority to appoint ministers, or whether that power should be returned to the Caucus.[118]

- Labor form a joint committee with the ACTU to coordinate campaign activities.

- Agreements should be negotiated with environmental, student and welfare groups to jointly run campaigns, carry out research and

---

[114] Troy Bramston, "ALP told to listen to party elders in 2010 Labor national review report," *The Australian*, 24 February 2011.
[115] Ibid.
[116] Ibid.
[117] Ibid.
[118] Ibid.

discuss policy.

The second section, which dealt with the 2010 campaign under Gillard's leadership (and ongoing campaigning), included the following recommendations:

- Develop a specific strategy to target voters lost to the Greens by advocating action on climate change and support for gay marriage, and to improve communication of Labor's "history of successful progressive reform" in targeted seats.

- Undertake research on the changing demographics of Labor's "base vote", particularly declining support in non-English speaking communities and among voters attracted to the Greens whose primary vote rose to a record 11.8 per cent at the last election.

- Develop stronger ties to the ACTU over campaigning and targeting union members.[119]

The national executive was to consider the 2010 Review's report and its recommendations at its April 2011 meeting.

2011 National Conference

Only 13 of the 2010 Review's 31 publicly released recommendations were fully adopted by the 2011 National Conference. Some were partly adopted, others were rejected outright. The recommendations adopted included conducting a national survey seeking member's views on the Party, suggestions on improving the Party's structure, and setting a target for membership growth. Those partly adopted included directly electing Party members from local branches to national conference.[120]

---

[119] Another was to review the Party's research program and much-criticised use of focus groups.

[120] The left pushed for 50 per cent of delegates to be directly elected by members, with union leaders to appoint the other 50 per cent..

It was resolved to implement this "landmark" reform by 2013, but without agreeing on a model for doing so; instead, it was left to the factions' leaders to sort out a deal at a later date – but nothing came of it.[121] Those recommendations rejected included; making the national president a voting member of the national executive;[122] a trial of community preselections; and restricting interventions by the national executive and state administrative committees.

2015 National Conference

The 2015 National Conference continued the push for affirmative action for women by adopting a new target which provided that from 2022 45 per cent of members of parliament must be women (up from 40 per cent), rising to 50 per cent in 2025. Conference also resolved that members directly elect 150 delegates to future national conferences. But there was no agreement on a motion to reform Senate preselections. The left argued for giving members in each State 50 per cent of the vote, and unions the other 50 per cent.[123] Having previously backed a say for members in Senate preselections, Labor leader Bill Shorten was reported to have been "accused of 'standing very, very still' on his pledge".[124] The left had also foreshadowed that it would push for the president and the two vice presidents to be given a vote on the national executive, which would have effectively given the left control

---

[121] Prime Minister Gillard (who put no number to her amendment) referred the issue to the "Implementation Committee" for discussion.

[122] The right opposed giving the president and the two vice presidents a vote on the national executive.

[123] This would have replaced the existing system under which Senate candidates were voted on by state conferences. Under this system, Labor Minister Penny Wong was placed behind little-known numbers man Don Farrell on Labor's South Australia ticket.

[124] Mathew Knott and Adam. Gatrell, "The six big issues to be debated at Labor's national conference," *Sydney Morning Herald*, 24 July 2015.

of what is the Party's most powerful governing body for the first time since the 1960s and 1970s. The right opposed the left's proposition; it never made it to the floor of Conference. It was resolved that a review of the Socialist Objective be conducted with a view to rewriting it.

4

THE REVIEWS' IMPACT ON THE PARTY'S STRUCTURE

For Anika Gauja:

> [T]he essence of [party] reform is that it is driven by the need for improvement and is intentionally publicised, and therefore it is more likely that reforms will concern major rather than minor organisational changes. Reforms need not necessarily involve formal rule changes …, but given the significance of these events, it might be expected that the majority of reforms would involve rule changes.[125]

This chapter analyses the internal Party debate, and public commentary by the media and academe, surrounding the two most recent Reviews' deliberations and recommendations on changes to the Party's structure (including coverage of the resolutions of rules and national conferences to which the Reviews' recommendations necessitating rule changes were referred), so as to focus attention on the state of the Party's structure at the outset of the 21st century. The chapter then consider the Party's structure going forward.

---

[125] Anika Gauja, *Party reform: the causes, challenges, and consequences of organizational change* (Oxford University Press, 2016), p 20.

The Party's structure at the outset of the 21st Century

Three major structural issues were debated and commented on in all the Reviews' deliberations and recommendations, but most importantly for the ALP's future are those that featured in the two Reviews conducted in the first decade of the twenty first century. The 2002 Review's recommendations concerning the Party's structure focused on reducing union representation at state conferences, but also on member direct election to national conference. The debate and commentary surrounding the 2010 Review focused on the dramatic decline in the Party's membership, with two main theories put forward as to its cause, while an academic suggestion held that concerns relying on formal membership alone would likely be "exaggerated". The 2011 and 2015 National Conferences focused on introducing direct elections for member delegates to national conference.

2002 Review: Branch stacking and union representation

Urgent calls for reform of the factions were being heard from those within the Party, such as Chris Schacht, a Minister in the Keating Government, who said if branch stacking were allowed to continue it would "hollow out" Labor; it would mean no grass roots organisation in the future.[126] As to the timing of these internal calls, what was different about the branch stacking of the 1990s was that it starts to be in the hundreds or even thousands.[127]

Coghlan and Denton conceded that Hawke and Wran had acknowledged that branch stacking was the cancerous effect of factionalism, and that it had the most alienating and detrimental effect

---

[126] Chris Schacht, 20 November, 2002.
[127] Rodney Cavalier et al., interview by Liz. Jackson2002.

on preselections, but they had focused on its "potential to damage the Party's electoral fortunes", rather than "as a cause and effect of factionalism".[128] Their "inability to recognise that the problems associated with branch stacking ran deeper than electoral fortunes indicated a naive response to an endemic decades-long problem".[129] Hawke and Wran also failed to acknowledge the practice of ethnic branch stacking, "the mass recruitment of ethnic-based memberships in order to assert control over a branch".[130] Kenneth Davidson, a writer for *The Age* on economic and public policy, argued that the process put up by the 2002 Review to reduce branch stacking was "minimalist".[131] However, Crean said the 2002 Review "gives us recommendations to weed out the branch stackers, and that I think, is fundamental in restoring integrity, trust, with the Australian people".[132] The 2010 Review bore out Crean's contention, noting branch stacking had largely been curtailed.

Wran said of the unions' relationship with the Party that "we shouldn't be tearing each other apart on an issue ... the general public doesn't understand". He didn't know what all the fuss was about over 60-40; it did not matter. "The unions were an integral part of the Labor movement, and whether it be 60-40 or 50-50, they'd remain an integral part of the Labor movement."[133] Wran's view was not shared by Rodney Cavalier, a Minister in the Wran Governments, who was scathing in his criticism of Hawke's and his former boss' report's view on unions.

---

[128] Coghlan and Denton, "Reviewing Labor's Internal Reviews 1966-2010: 'Looking forward, looking backwards'," p 31.
[129] Ibid.
[130] Ibid., p 32.
[131] Kenneth. Davidson, "Flimsy whimsy of Hawke and Wran won't save Labor," *The Age*, 12 August 2002.
[132] Crean et al., "Crean to fight for Hawke-Wran proposals."
[133] Ibid.

> I find it amazing that an *equal partnership* is required between those
> who represent the vast mass of the Australian people and those
> who represent that sliver of the workforce who are unionised [italics
> added]… 75 per cent of workers are not in unions, 85 per cent to 88
> per cent are not in unions affiliated to the ALP, and I really think it's
> a departure from reality to assert that the university graduates and
> the university dropouts who are cased to come in and take on union
> positions have any connection with working Australia at all.[134]

Coughlan and Denton contended that union representation at state conferences was more an issue for Party "oligarchs" and factional leaders than for Party members.[135] Davidson argued that the 2002 Review's unstated, primary purpose was to improve the electability of the current "oligarchy" – politicians such as Party leader Simon Crean – without undermining its power. The "oligarchy" had no intention of giving real power over policy back to members. Anyway, reducing union representation at state conferences would be largely cosmetic, as the factions were the real barrier to restoring Labor's democratic traditions.[136]

In the opinion of Frank Bongiorno, transforming the Party conferences into occasions for real debate about ideas and policies (rather than arenas where backroom deals by factional heavyweights are rubber-stamped by delegates) was a more critical issue than debate over whether the 60-40 rule gave affiliated unions undue representation at Party conferences.[137] He noted that union influence had been vigorously debated inside and outside the labour movement

[134] Cavalier et al., "Simon Says: Federal Labor's crisis of confidence and how Simon Crean is dealing with it ".
[135] Coghlan and Denton, "Reviewing Labor's Internal Reviews 1966-2010: 'Looking forward, looking backwards'," pp 33-4.
[136] Davidson, "Flimsy whimsy of Hawke and Wran won't save Labor."
[137] Frank Bongiorno, "The end of the affair?: Unions, citizens and the future of the ALP," *Australian Review of Public Affairs* (2002). Although he accepts that "like any other aspect of the Party's organisation, the 60-40 rule should be subject to debate".

since the 2001 election, and has been one of the most persistent features of the Party's history.[138] Bongiorno also argued that "whatever the causes of Labor's failure to displace the Howard Government, union domination of the Party seems an unlikely explanation."[139] But a decade after the 2002 Review's report was released; Coghlan and Denton argued that the 2002 Review in large part blamed unions for the unelectable position of the ALP in the post-2001 political environment.[140] This notwithstanding the 2002 Review's report found there was no evidence the unions were a liability for Labor at the 2001 election.

Crean, in a speech to the 2002 National Left Conference, said reducing union voting rights within the Party was a "perception issue"; it was not that Labor would not have relationships with the union movement, but we have to "build relationships with other constituencies".[141]

The response of the union movement to the 2002 Review's report was generally positive. The National Secretary of the SDA, Joe de Bruyn, said the "report was strong on the relationship between Labor and the unions, and arguably strengthens the position of the unions in the Labor Party."[142] But de Bruyn was "disappointed" with the recommendation that union representation at state conferences

---

[138]   Ibid. He went on to say: "In the modern ALP, unaffiliated unions—many of them white-collar—are also part of the equation. Their affiliation with the ACTU gives them special access to the ALP, while many active members of these unions also belong to the ALP through local branches."

[139]   Ibid.

[140]   Jo Coghlan and Scott Denton, "The irony of the ACTU's defence of the ALP," (On Line Opinion, 2012).

[141]   Simon Crean, "ALP must modernise and be more inclusive" (paper presented at the ALP National Left Conference, 2002).

[142]   Darren Gray and Sophie Douez, "Unions back the thrust of Hawke, Wran report," *The Age*, 10 August 2002.

be dropped from 60 to 50 per cent.[143] He also thought that Crean showed poor political judgement in focusing on internal Party reform, which (other than de Bruyn's criticism of Crean's judgement) was not dissimilar to Wran's comments.[144] The ACTU's Secretary, Greg Combet, said "[i]t's our hope that shortly, the debate about the ALP's structure can be put behind us."[145]

According to Coghlan and Denton, the Party's relationship with the unions was hardly raised in submissions. "More [submissions] were concerned with changing the quota system ensuring 50% of all Labor parliamentarians were women".[146] On the ABC's *PM*, Louise Yaxley said a "proposal to boost the quota from 35 per cent to 50 per cent was dropped from the Hawke-Wran review as part of a factional deal."[147] And in an interview with Crean on the ABC's *The World Today*,[148] the interviewer Alexandra Kirk said that the Labor women's lobby were "angered" by the 2002 Review's failure to recommend a more ambitious quota. Former Victorian Premier Joan Kirner was "disappointed".[149] In his commentary, Davidson made the point that affirmative action to ensure a certain proportion of women were preselected for safe seats cut across the ALP's declared aim of democratising the Party.[150]

[143] Ibid.
[144] Ibid.
[145] Ibid.
[146] Coghlan and Denton, "Reviewing Labor's Internal Reviews 1966-2010: 'Looking forward, looking backwards'," p 31.
[147] Crean et al., "Crean to fight for Hawke-Wran proposals."
[148] Simon Crean, interview by Alexandra Kirk, 9 August, 2002.
[149] Crean et al., "Crean to fight for Hawke-Wran proposals."
[150] Davidson, "Flimsy whimsy of Hawke and Wran won't save Labor."

2002 Rules Conference: Union representation and member direct election

The 2002 Review's recommendations requiring rule changes formed the basis of the 2002 Rules Conference's terms of reference. More than the 2011 and 2015 National Conferences, the 2002 Rules Conference was the subject of internal Party criticism and recriminations.

Crean supported the Hawke-Wran report's call for a reduction in union representation at state conferences from 60:40 to 50:50. Crean, as parliamentary leader, put the case for the rule change. Federal Members of Parliament from NSW Mark Latham and Joel Fitzgibbon spoke in support of the motion; John Robertson from the NSW Labour Council and Senator Steve Hutchins (a former Federal President of the TWU) from NSW spoke against it. Crean won the vote 121 to 69, due largely to the left's 85 votes. But there was also division within NSW centre unity politicians, with Premier Bob Carr supporting Crean, while two of his more influential ministers, Special Minister of State John Della Bosca (a former NSW Party General Secretary) and Police Minister Michael Costa (a former Secretary of the NSW Labour Council), voted against Crean. All State Premiers and Territory Chief Ministers supported Crean.[151] Chris Christodoulou, the left's Assistant Secretary of the NSW Labour Council, said the resolution to reduce unions' representation at state conferences was a "symbolic thing" that Crean wanted, and "people ... thought that if they didn't support the leader on that issue, that we might find ourselves with a situation where we need to find a new leader on the

---

[151] Fia Cumming and Andrew West, "ALP: It's time for reform," *Sydney Morning Herald*, 6 October 2002.

Monday after the Conference".[152]

However, the internal Party debate was more taken up with the Hawke-Wran report's recommendation for member direct election to national conference, which the factions came together on to defeat. Lindsay Tanner, Minister for Finance and Deregulation in the Gillard and Rudd Governments, said "[w]e should have introduced direct election for National Conference delegates to ensure that Party members feel involved, feel they're treated more seriously, feel as if they have some say in the process that leads to a Labor Government's platform."[153] Tanner attributed the failure to pass a resolution for member direct election to a "mixture of self-interest, of fear, of, in some respects, cynicism about the potential outcome".[154]

Crean strongly disagreed with Tanner. Direct election to national conference did not, of itself, give more members a say in the decision-making processes of the Party "[b]ecause people having to get elected to national conference would have to have gotten so many local votes, it would have made sure that not many at all got up as rank and filers."[155]

Encel offered some historical perspective when in 2004 he recalled that one of the 1979 Inquiry's "central proposals" was "direct election of rank-and-file members from each Federal Electorate Council to the national conference.[156] This proposal, as Button sardonically observed, threatened too many hostile fiefdoms."[157] As a member of

---

[152] Cavalier et al., "Simon Says: Federal Labor's crisis of confidence and how Simon Crean is dealing with it ". Christodoulou also said that any new leader might have been less sympathetic to the unions.
[153] Ibid.
[154] Ibid.
[155] Ibid.
[156] Encel, "Labor and the Future: Where to now?."
[157] Ibid.

the 1979 Inquiry, Encel had been "dispatched to address the NSW executive, and the hostility in the room was palpable, not least from the recently appointed State Secretary, Graham Richardson".[158]

2010 Review: The dramatic decline in the Party's membership

In the eight years leading up to the 2010 Review, the focus on structural reform had shifted from union control of the Party to a dramatic decline in the Party's membership. But Coghlan and Denton argued that the 2010 Review's analysis "hardly informs why the Labor Party struggled to staff polling booths, nor explains why branch members are not participating".[159]

Cavalier wrote that the Party "is beset by a crisis of belief, a crisis of purpose" that makes [the 2010 Review] different from all previous internal reviews. Now is the time for a self-examination that asks existential questions."[160] Is there any point in joining a political party if the members play no role in campaigns, candidate selection and policy formation? He predicted that, without a major transfer of power from the unions to the membership, "it is an actuarial certainty that the only membership remaining in 20 years will be those in jobs dependent on loyalty to Labor".[161] However, William Cross and Gauja argued there had been few signs of deterioration in the ALP's membership's three "procedural functions" raised by Cavalier.[162] They noted Katz's argument that the "decline in membership numbers may have little to

---

[158] Ibid.
[159] Coghlan and Denton, "Reviewing Labor's Internal Reviews 1966-2010: 'Looking forward, looking backwards'," p 35.
[160] Rodney Cavalier, *The Australian*, 13 October 2010.
[161] Ibid.
[162] William Cross and Anika Gauja, "Evolving membership strategies in Australian political parties," *Australian Journal of Political Science* 49, no. 4 (2014): p 612.

do with the ways in which parties operate internally and may instead reflect broader societal changes that are completely exogenous to questions of Party organisation",[163] with people no longer joining religious, sporting and other social clubs in large numbers. Still, Katz and Mair warn that political parties lacking a firm social base in society are potentially vulnerable.[164]

However, more significantly for Cross and Gauja was their claim that "membership is a flexible concept",[165] and that "accounts of Party decline which rely on formal membership alone", such as Cavalier's and Katz's, "are likely exaggerated."[166] They argue that "members constitute a 'go to' group, but donors, volunteers and ambassadors are just as valuable to Australian political parties."[167] They approvingly quote the view that "the experiences of Rainbow Labor created a model of *modern membership* that successfully fits within existing Party structures while reaching beyond traditional notions of formal, branch-based members [italics added]".[168] They go on, "[a] more *diverse* notion of what it means to be a Party member is evident in the ... experience of successful intra-Party *advocacy groups*, such as Rainbow Labor [italics added]".[169] Yet the ALP also "knows that if it gives away too much *authority* it risks being *captive* to the more ideologically extreme elements among its supporters who are likely to be the most active (as was the case with UK Labour in the 1970s and 1980s) [italics added]."[170] In a similar vein, Bongiorno suggests

[163] Ibid., p 613.
[164] Richard Katz and Peter Mair, "Changing Models of Party Organization and Party Democracy: The Emergence of the Cartel Party," *Party Politics* 1, no. 1 (1995): pp 26-28.
[165] Cross and Gauja, "Evolving membership strategies in Australian political parties," p 612.
[166] Ibid., pp 623-4.
[167] Ibid., p 619.
[168] Ibid., p 618.
[169] Ibid., pp 622-3.
[170] Ibid., pp 623-4.

the Party become more "open to involvement by environmentalists, Indigenous Australians, enthusiasts for Reconciliation, women's groups, advocates of public schools, and others", but without leaving itself open to the accusation that it is a "*captive* of 'special interest groups' or 'elites' [italics added]". Bongiorno contends that "Labor must tap into these forms of community activism if it is going to be much more than a professional vote-catching outfit".[171]

Gary Johns, a Minister in the Keating Government, warned that "[a]llowing the affiliation of *like-minded organisations* would potentially allow hundreds of nongovernment organisations into the ALP. These would swamp the membership, in effect turning it into the Greens. [italics addred]"[172] Johns would know about the influence of "like-minded organisations" on Labor governments, for as Bongiorno noted it was accusations it was "captive" of special interest groups and elites that "helped to sink the Keating government".[173]

However, it is not necessary, as Cross and Gauja imply, that "ideological extremists" within the interest groups "capture" the Party; it is sufficient that activists involved with interest groups are granted "authority" over Labor's policies. This does not necessitate affiliation to the Party (as Johns warns against allowing). For while interest groups are not affiliated to the Party, they are unofficially recognised by it. Further, while they are not delegates to national or state conferences, and so cannot themselves place items on the agenda, they can have items placed on state agendas by orchestrating the passing of motions at local and policy branches, FECs, SECs and on the NPF, with the motions to be forwarded to state head offices

---

[171] Bongiorno, "The end of the affair?: Unions, citizens and the future of the ALP."
[172] Gary Johns, "Labor risks taking its democracy too far," *The Australian*, 8 December 2011.
[173] Bongiorno, "The end of the affair?: Unions, citizens and the future of the ALP."

to be placed on state conference agendas. Flooding state head offices with motions this way is a favourite tactic of LEAN. Activists also lobby Ministers or Shadow Ministers.

The unions had little to say on the Party's membership; rather, in a more cautious media release than suggested by its title *Labor Party reaffirms unions as the "bedrock" of the modern ALP*, the ACTU's Secretary Jeff Lawrence said "[u]nions and the ACTU will examine the Bracks-Carr-Faulkner review in more detail in coming days, but our initial reaction is positive about the role and relationship of the union movement to Labor".[174] ACTU President Ged Kearney was still more circumspect, saying that "[u]nions will not always see eye to eye with Labor, and in recent years as throughout history there have been points of conflict".[175]

2011 and 2015 National Conferences: Member direct election

One of Australia's leading political journalists and authors, Laurie Oakes, wrote on the Saturday of the 2011 National Conference that no one in a position of power is prepared to risk all, as did Whitlam in the 1960s. Now Labor needs reforming again. Oakes believed that "[t]o renew itself, Labor must attract new members, it must give the rank and file a say in decisions. ... Members must feel they have ownership of the Party".[176] Rank and file election of the national executive, national conference and the parliamentary leader "would provide the kind of shake-up Labor needs". But there was little chance

---

[174] ACTU, "Labor Party review reaffirms unions as the "bedrock" of the modern ALP," news release, 18 February, 2011.

[175] Ibid.

[176] Laurie Oakes, "Reforms needed or Labor will die," *The Daily Telegraph*, 3 December 2011.

the "ALP conference will do more than fiddle around the edges".[177] Oakes thought the factional bosses, and the 400 delegates who dance to their tune, are going to squib the crisis of "Labor's long-term survival as a major political force". They will simply "put it off for another day, by which time things will be even more desperate".[178] All Oakes thought might get up was a "minor breakthrough": giving Party president, Jenny McAllister, a vote on the national executive. And although the president presides over meetings of the national executive, it is a position without any real power.[179] He caustically remarked that "a genuine solution would involve those who wield power giving some of it up. They are unwilling to do so."[180]

Writing at the time of the 2015 National Conference, ALP historian and political columnist, Troy Bramston, was sure that, "[a]lthough union membership will no longer be a requirement of Party membership, Labor remains firmly in the grip of unions. The advice of Party and union elders to recast the relationship has fallen on deaf ears."[181] Bramston reported on former ACTU Secretary Bill Kelty (who worked with Bob Hawke and Paul Keating in the 1980s and 90s on the Accord between government and unions) saying to Party activists at the Victorian Trades Hall that "it was time for unions to cede power to Party members. 'Unions are an integral and important part of [the ALP union relationship], but they can never own it,' he said. 'Nobody should ever aspire to ever own [the Party]'."[182] Yet for Bramston, "unions seem to think it is their Party". He was in no doubt that "unions still dominate the Party. Reforming the Party-union nexus

---

[177]   Ibid.

[178]   Ibid.

[179]   Ibid.

[180]   Ibid.

[181]   Troy Bramston, "ALP Conference 2015: unions still rule OK, despite minor reforms," *The Australian*, 27 July 2015.

[182]   Ibid.

must remain on the agenda for future conferences".[183] Bramston highlighted a certain inconsistency in the proposal of the AMWU's NSW Branch Secretary, Tim Ayers, to wit "union delegates to state conferences be given a 50 per cent say in Senate preselections and in the election of national conference delegates. This would be weighted equally against the votes of rank and file Party members." But this proposal would mean that in NSW the votes of approximately 20,000 members would be equally weighted against 400 union delegates appointed by 22 union secretaries. As Bramston caustically put it, "Ayres thinks the Party should democratise, but not unions."[184]

However, Bramston also reported approvingly that there was "some organisational reform" at Conference. [185] Members will now directly elect 150 delegates to national conference, and a new gender equity quota of 50 per cent of parliamentary seats by 2025 was adopted.

The Party's structure going forward

As discussed above, according to the 2010 Review branch stacking has fallen away as a concern for the Party, while the role of factions was virtually unquestioned by either the 2002 or 2010 Review. As is clear from the 2002 Review, the 2002 Rules, the 2011and 2015 National Conferences, the unions have to date retained their grip on power within the Party, although the 2015 National Conference resolved that 150 members would be directly elected to national conference. Commentary on the dramatic decline in Party membership focused on whether it was caused by an unrepresentative Party structure or broad societal change, and on an academic suggestion for "advocacy

---

[183] Ibid.
[184] Ibid.
[185] Ibid.

groups" to be part of a "modern membership". Clearly these three major structural issues have yet to be resolved, and as such they warrant more in depth consideration here. What has become of the factions? Will the unions be able to maintain their control of the Party in the face of calls for further reductions in their representation at state conferences, and what are the electoral implications for Labor from the parlous state of the Party's membership?

Factions then and now

Organised factions have existed within the ALP from as early as 1916 in NSW. However, other tensions surface within the ALP from time to time, including those between the federal parliamentary leader and the Party; between the parliamentary and organisational wings; between state branches and between groups of affiliated trade unions. However, the Party's factions are the most enduring divisions, and affect the way these other tensions play out. Formalised factions are not unique to the ALP's state and federal politics. They have a history in UK Labour, and exist in many western social democratic parties, such as Germany's SPD and Italy's PD. A difference being that the ALP's factions are more structured than those of Western Europe, or in the other Australian political parties.

As a consequence of the 1970-71 federal interventions in the NSW and Victorian Branches that compelled these states to enter into power sharing arrangements, "winner take all" ballots were replaced by "proportional representation" at state conferences. Proportional representation formalised factional behaviour. It did not reduce factional activity; it increased it. From 1971 onwards, proportional representation forced operatives in each state branch to organise themselves into factions, and for those factions to form voting blocs at national conference with like-minded factions from other states and territories. But it was not until 1981 that the Party openly admitted to the existence of factions. On being elected President of NSW Labor in 1979, Paul Keating announced the existence of a right faction – which he renamed centre unity – saying it would operate openly.[186] By the early 1980s, the three main factions – right, left and centre-left – had been formed in most states.[187] However, a centre-left faction never formed in NSW, although there were breakaway groupings from the left and right, but they did not last. The factions held scheduled meetings, had rules, published newsletters, developed policies on some issues, elected officers and appointed negotiators to do inter-factional deals. Their convenors emerged as power brokers – the so-called "machine men". A year after Bob Hawke led the ALP to victory in 1983, the supporters of the deposed parliamentary leader, Bill Hayden, formed a bloc in Caucus that melded into a national faction. They were some of the most able members of the Hawke Ministry – such as John Button, Michael Duffy, Peter Walsh and John Dawkins[188] – all of whom enjoyed the strong backing of their state branches of Victoria and WA. The formation of this "anti-faction" provided the motivation for many of the state-based left and right factions to do the same.[189]

The factions agreed to power sharing arrangements nationally. As part of which, whereas previously appointments to the front bench, outer ministry and parliamentary committees were decided by open ballot within the Caucus, the factions would in future be allocated

[186] Cavalier, *Power Crisis: The Self-destruction of a State Labor Party*, p 37.
[187] Graham Richardson, *Whatever It Takes* (Sydney, NSW: Bantam, 1994), p 80.
[188] The Hawke Government's economic agenda was in large part put in place by these influential Shadow Ministers appointed by Hayden when Opposition Leader, all of whom understood first-hand the failings of the Whitlam Government.
[189] Clem Lloyd, "A quest for national rules," in *The Machine: Labor confronts the future*, ed. John. Warhurst and Andrew. Parkin (St Leonards, NSW: Allen & Unwin, 2000), p 57.

ministerial and committee chair positions based on their representation in Caucus. Each faction would then choose from within their ranks the Members of the House of Representatives and Senators who would fill those positions. The procedure involved each factional Caucus meeting to endorse their candidates, with individual votes checked by factional overseers before being placed in the ballot box. All that would remain for Caucus would be to rubber-stamp what had already been agreed.[190] The parliamentary leader would then allocate portfolios. The Hawke ministry was the first to be negotiated by the factions. Their convenors, NSW centre unity power broker Graham Richardson, Robert Ray, Gerry Hand from the left and Peter Cook from the centre-left commanded respect in Caucus. They built relationships, agreed to promote the most able, and worked for the good of the government. But as the factions tightened their hold on the Party during Labor's time in office from 1983 to 1996, promotion of the most able became a thing of the past.[191] Bob Hawke was to say later that "the factions [had] broken down into smaller parts, into fiefdoms, and [it was] more about power".[192]

Or as Ray put it in 2006, there has been a "balkanisation" of the major factions, now they are more about shifting alliances of unions and political personalities than ideology;[193] neither the left nor the right faction is a unifying force. Ray also pointed to the factions' trend to hegemony, "leaving no opportunity for talented Labor Party members who have no factional allegiance".[194] In his 2013 book *A Letter to Generation Next: Why Labor*, Kim Carr claimed that the factions are at their worst when they "become nothing more than a vehicle for

---

[190] Paul Kelly, *The End of Certainty: Power, Politics and Business in Australia* (St. Leonards, NSW: Allen & Unwin, 1994), p 30.

[191] Cavalier, *Power Crisis: The Self-destruction of a State Labor Party*, pp 37-38.

[192] Crean et al., "Crean to fight for Hawke-Wran proposals."

[193] Robert Ray, "Are Factions Killing the Labor Party?," in *Address to the Fabian Society* (Sydney 2006).

[194] Ibid.

the distribution of patronage. And ... that [is what] predominates in public opinion."[195]

But could the factions again take on the constructive role they did in the early years of the Hawke Government. To again be, as Carr claimed they once were, instruments for the "nurturing of a culture in which members can realise their potential, by forming a protective arena in which a diversity of ideas can flourish, assumptions can be challenged and debate encouraged? [196] For at its best, claimed Carr, the factional system "allows that to happen – when it marries ideas with numbers, and when numbers are used to empower ideas."[197]

For that to happen, Ray says that all the factions have to work for the Party, rather than against it.[198] His two part message is: "Today we must demand ... of factional leaders that they put *the Party's interest ahead of factional supremacy.*"[199] The second part is: "Federal renewal will only come from the FPLP – it will not come from the Party organisation, or ... the unions – it will come from the leadership and the inspiration of Federal Caucus. ... That will only take place when we have a Caucus brimming full with talent." [200] Ray urges factional leaders to go outside their own members when recruiting candidates for preselections.[201]

Ray was a senior minister in the Hawke Government, a right factional convenor from Victoria during the Hawke Government, and a member of the national executive from 1983-1998. Carr, Shadow Minister for Higher Education, Research, is a left powerbroker from

---

[195] Kim Carr, *A Letter to Generation Next: Why Labor* (Carlton, Vic.: Melbourne University Press, 2013), p 36.

[196] Ibid., p 35.

[197] Ibid., p 36.

[198] Ray, "Are Factions Killing the Labor Party?."

[199] Ibid.

[200] Ibid.

[201] Ibid.

Victoria, and has been a member of the national executive since1994 (he is the longest serving member of the national executive). Ray and Carr have been intimately involved in factional politics at the highest level from the Hawke Government to the present.

Dyrenfurth, quoting former WA Labor Premier turned academic Geoff Gallop, questioned the "potential for organised factions to lead the Party's intellectual renewal".[202] The left faction is not all that important; "[h]istory shows that the Party is unlikely to renew its purpose without the Right's imprimatur."[203] But with the fall of communism and collapse of leftist ideological opponents, the right lost the "glue" that had held its members[204] together. Significantly, too, from early in the 1970s on there had been the "decline of Catholicism as an animating political force in the lives of Right figures."[205] Then in the 1980s, the right "buttressed" the Hawke-Keating government's economic reform agenda,[206] which "bequeathed Australia with three decades of economic growth".[207] Bongiorno argues that "the Right was always a very NSW and Sydney-centric affair"[208] (although centre unity also controls branches in NSW country that the left does not contest). Michael Easson, a former Secretary of the NSW Labour Council, is empathetic: the NSW Right is the "grand old faction

---

[202] Nick Dyrenfurth, "Labor's damaged Right faction must renew," *The Saturday Paper*, 18 April 2015 2015.

[203] Ibid.

[204] These members were the "'brothers'– later 'mates'– who firmly controlled the Party machine and acquired a reputation for political pragmatism and social conservatism." Ibid.

[205] Ibid.

[206] Dyrenfurth refers to this as Labor's "new big idea: a historic rebalancing of state and market forces that emptied out much of the labourist model by virtue of floating the dollar, financial market deregulation, dismantling tariffs, privatising public assets and, in 1993, introducing a form of enterprise bargaining that heralded a major shift away from centralised wage-fixing."

[207] Dyrenfurth, "Labor's damaged Right faction must renew."

[208] Quoted in ibid.

that kept Gough Whitlam in the Party in the 1960s, co-opted Bob Hawke … and created Paul Keating. Across 70 years, a string of NSW premiers came from this group or were co-opted into it."[209]

However, Dyrenfurth identifies failings within NSW centre unity of late, in that it has suffered from a "perception" of moral decline. Richo's creed of "whatever it takes" seems to now mean "whatever we can take", as evidenced by the behaviour of National President Michael Williamson, federal parliamentarian Craig Thomson and state parliamentarians Joe Tripodi and Eddie Obeid. Centre unity retains its dominance in NSW, [210] although its standing nationally has been "damaged";[211] it no longer enjoys preferential rights to parliamentary leadership at either the state or federal level. Another, related, failing of NSW centre unity is its lack of a coherent narrative about what it stands for. Dyrenfurth quotes Paul Keating as saying: "I think the problem with centre unity in NSW is that it lacks now an ideology … other than the sheer pursuit of power … But power for what?" "There is little sign of the intellectual and organisational renewal required [for NSW centre unity] to regain its potency."[212]

As for Dyrenfurth's claim that the left faction lacks importance when it comes to intellectual renewal; Peter Baldwin, a Minister in the Hawke and Keating Governments who was from the NSW left, warns of the threat posed to Labor from the "renewal" being foisted on the Party by today's left-wing, progressives. In a 2016 article, Baldwin asked rhetorically: "What does it mean, these days,

---

[209] Michael. Easson, "The Right approach for a tired organisation," *The Weekend Australian*, 8-9 December 2012.

[210] In that it maintains a majority of union and other delegates to the NSW state conference, and hence delegates to national conference and membership of the national executive.

[211] Mostly by evidence at ICAC hearings, and subsequent sentencing of Obeid to five years jail for misconduct in public office.

[212] Dyrenfurth, "Labor's damaged Right faction must renew."

when someone says their politics are 'left-wing' or 'progressive'? …This has always been debatable, but in recent times these terms have taken on meanings that earlier generations of leftists would scarcely recognise. Ideas that used to be thought constitutive of left-wing thinking have been turned on their head." Baldwin traces this turning to a "comprehensive rejection by *progressive academe* of the intellectual inheritance from the Enlightenment", such that today the "'Enlightenment project', as they now style it, is typically disparaged by intellectuals of a progressive bent [italics added]."[213] Baldwin uses the term "regressive left", coined in the US and UK, to describe an element of the left who are "tolerant" of illiberal ideologies – in particular, Islamism in support of multiculturalism. Baldwin identifies the:

> substantive content of [their] ideology [as] *identity politics*, the view that people should be seen in their essence not as members of a common humanity but as bound to a particular identity group. … [T]he compliance and enforcement arm is the system of thought control we nowadays term *political correctness* … [there is a] hierarchy of correctness in which cultural respect is trumps [italics added].[214]

The term identity politics has been used in academic discourse since at least the 1970s, aspects of which can be seen in many of the earliest writings of feminists, multiculturalists, and gay and lesbian activists. During the 1980s, it gained prominence, becoming

---

[213]   Peter. Baldwin, "Regressive Left puts bigotry and militant Islam on a pedestal," *The Australian*, 17 September 2016.

[214]   Ibid. Matt Ridley, writing in *The Times*, argues that left right politics has reached a tipping point. "The Left has vacated the moral high ground on which it won so many fine battles to treat human beings equally. The right must occupy that ground and stand for universal human values and equal treatment for all." Matt Ridley, "Left is creating a new kind of apartheid," *The Times*, 28 November 2016.

associated with a new wave of social movements.[215] Moreover, whereas previously only a minority of left academics in Social Sciences and Humanities were adherents of Marxism, today identity politics dominates "discourse" in these disciplines. The political significance of this radicalisation of academe lies in its influence on university graduates (in the literate disciplines more so than in the numerate sciences) who are disproportionally represented in the professions, such as politics, law, business, human resource management, the arts, teaching and the media, and thus are in positions from which to undermine Western values.

The distinguished journalist and author Paul Kelly warned of the chilling effect identity politics is having on public dialogue and debate in Australia when he wrote that many of the country's institutions and prominent figures "buckle before the campaigns of identity politics, too weak to stand on principle," as breaking its rules "risks being branded a racist or sexist."[216]

Succumbing to identity politics has other consequences. The pressing economic problems of the day that required urgent attention were dealt with by Hawke and Keating. It is politically more difficult coming up with solutions to today's economic problems, such as a stagnant economy, weak wages growth, poor productivity, high structural unemployment, welfare reform, the Henry Tax Review

---

[215] See Craig Calhoun, *Social Theory and the Politics of Identity* (Blackwell, 1994).

[216] Paul Kelly, "Race, gender: the risk of identity politics," *The Australian*, 6 August 2016. Kelly gave as an example the plebiscite on same-sex marriage, which he wrote: "constitutes a seismic shift in our politics and testifies to the power of identity politics. An expression of popular will and democratic sentiment cannot be conducted because it will give *offence*. ... The power of the argument is immense — witness Shorten railing in the campaign against the plebiscite, saying it would release hate and homophobia. Forget any benefit from having the people express their views. Forget the legitimacy involved in having the people settle the issue — the plebiscite cannot be tolerated because it causes *offence* [italics added]."

(e.g. corporate taxation and tax evasion), structural problems with the budget (e.g. middle class welfare and an ageing population), and conflicting Commonwealth and State energy policies. These issues have no easy solutions, no political winners, only painful trade-offs. "Focusing on *identity* is simply easier than coming up with original ideas or workable policies [italics added]."[217]

Crucially for Labor, columnist and author Owen Jones argues that the triumph of identity politics is causing a fundamental problem for UK Labour. For while the "struggles for the emancipation of women, gays and ethnic minorities are exceptionally important causes", these agendas have "happily co-existed with the sidelining of the working class in politics allowing [UK Labour] to protect its radical [left] flank.[218] This is not only a problem for the UK; it is happening "[a]cross the whole of the left ... There has been a drift away from class politics towards *identity politics* over the last thirty years [italics added]."[219]

Cavalier also attributes the degeneration of the factions to the ending of the cold war, as when he wrote of their having "lost their connection with ideology or the realm of ideas ..."[220] However, Cavalier's concern is not Party renewal; rather, it is that the loss of ideology has in part led to the rise in the 1980s of a "political class".[221] In his lecture, "Politics as a Vocation", Max Weber said of

---

217 Claire Lehmann, "We must resist the scourge of 'identity politics'," *The Drum* (2015). This is not to say Labor is devoid of economic reform initiatives. But as Peter van Onselen wrote: "the reform on the table (Labor's negative gearing and capital gains tax changes) or enacted (government legislation on superannuation and construction sector changes) are piecemeal at best". Peter van Onselen, "Reform-averse politicians are letting down the nation," *The Australian*, 10 December 2016.

218 Owen Jones, *Chavs: The Demonisation of the Working Class* (London, UK: Verso, 2012), p 255.

219 Ibid.

220 Cavalier, *Power Crisis: The Self-destruction of a State Labor Party*, p 38.

221 Ibid., p 50.

these people that they not only live "for politics" but their careers are made "off politics" as policy analysts and experts in specific fields.[222] Cavalier fingers as members "those on the staff of ministers, the ALP office and union officials who do not come from the industries their union represents".[223] Inside a generation "the political class moved toward a monopoly in candidate selection for any winnable seat ... The parliamentary [Labor Party] became the domain of the political class".[224] The rise of the political class has since the 1990s been facilitated by the practice of so-called "parachuting" (and "Captain's picks") of candidates into safe Labor seats ahead of pre-selection ballots by means of either the national executive's or the state's administrative committee's or executive's centralised imposition of candidates made at the request of the federal and state parliamentary leaders.

The consequences for government economic policy of the political class' prevalence among federal parliamentarians of the major political parties were spelled out by Peter Hartcher writing in the *Sydney Morning Herald*:

> Australia's economic rejuvenation under the Hawke and Keating governments, with some finishing touches from Howard and Costello, gave it an exceptionally flexible new structure. In the last quarter-century, Australia has grown undisturbed by the great traumas of our age – the 1997-98 Asian financial crisis, the 2001

---

[222] Max H. H. Gerth and C. Wright Mills, eds., *From Max Weber: Essays in Sociology* (New York: Oxford University Press, 1946), p 84.

[223] Moreover, as Tom Bramble and Rick Kuhn note, it has been "established since the early writings of Sidney and Beatrice Webb, full-time trade union officials experience rather different working and life circumstances to the workers by whom they are elected or they are appointed to serve". Tom Bramble and Rick Kuhn, "Continuity or Discontinuity in the Recent History of the Australian Labor Party?," *Australian Journal of Political Science* 44, no. 2 (2009): p 283

[224] Cavalier.

US recession, the 2008-09 global financial crisis.[225]

Today it's evidently beyond the "political class" to deal with some of our larger problems.[226]

Under the heading "Confidence in democracy hits record low as Australians 'disaffected with political class'", the ABC reported on the findings of a study of the 2016 federal election result conducted by the School of Politics and International Relations at the ANU covering dissatisfaction with political parties. Lead researcher, Professor Ian McAllister, was reported as saying that the election study was a wake-up call for Australia's political leadership. "What we are seeing in Australia are the beginnings of a popular disaffection with the *political class* that has emerged so dramatically in Britain [and in the] United States [italics added]."[227]

Cavalier argues that the rule changes required to scuttle the political class' ambitions within the Labor Party are brutal: an absolute prohibition on members of the political class standing for preselection for not less than five years since they were last so employed. Similar, if less "brutal", is Dyrenfurth's suggestion that the ALP "should … be able to cap the number of staffers, union officials and Party apparatchiks currently contesting and inexorable winning pre-selections."[228]

---

[225] Peter Hartcher, "Beholden to the cargo cult: Australia's political class letting us down," *Sydney Morning Herald* 15 December 2017.

[226] Ibid.

[227] Henry Belot, "Confidence in democracy hits record low as Australians 'disaffected with political class'", ABC News, Online. 20 December 2018.

[228] Nick Dyrenfurth, "It's time Labor went back to the workers," *The Weekend Australian*, 22-23 October 2011.

"You don't get me, I'm part of the union"[229]

Author of the authoritative work *The Split*, Robert Murray, wrote that in 1955 a "group of twenty-four 'pro-Evatt' [NSW] unions ... adopted ... a more formal organisation [than in Victoria]".[230] This led to a left group in NSW calling itself the Steering Committee being formed, essentially to act as an umbrella for those opposed to the Catholic Movement-dominated leadership of the ALP, and the role played from the late 1940s onwards by the Industrial Groups within the labour movement.[231] The 1980s witnessed the division of the Steering Committee into two hostile camps, which culminated in the 1989 intra-left split. The camps were referred to by various names. The most common being the "Cavalierites" or "soft left", and the "Walkerites" or "hard left". Initially the dispute was over ideology and tactics, but was soon exacerbated by personal animosities. The major ideological debate revolved around whether the left should support changes to the ratio in which unions and local branches were represented at state conference. Other ideological differences were the hard left's desire for closer links with left movements outside the ALP, such as peace, environment and some Marxist groups.[232] During the late 1970s and early 1980s, many of those who would form the soft left had argued that the left should support changing the ratio from 60:40 to 50:50, on the grounds that the numbers of union members were declining, and "unionists were becoming increasingly conservative".[233] The hard

---

[229] Strawbs: Part of the union, 1973.

[230] Robert Murray, *The Split : Australian Labor in the Fifties* (Sydney, NSW: Hale & Ironmonger, 1984), p 189.

[231] Rodney Cavalier, "The Australian Labor Party at Branch Level: Guildford, Hunters Hill and Panania Branches in the 1950s.," in *A Century of Social Change: Labor History Essays Volume Four*, ed. Australian Labor Party (1992), p 118.

[232] Also, the soft left had a more consensual approach towards dealing with the right on policy issues.

[233] Andrew Leigh, "Factions and Fractions: A Case Study of Power Politics in the Australian Labor Party," *Australian Journal of Political Science* 35, no. 3 (2000): p 437.

left opposed the idea, arguing that, as a matter of principle, the left should campaign to retain union representation at more than half of the delegates to state conference. The soft left's main support was in the ALP's branches, while the hard left's was in the trade unions. Any reduction in union representation would have hurt the hard left more than the soft left.

Today's leading advocates for reforming the ALP union relationship are former politicians from this NSW soft left, Cavalier and Faulkner. Now as then, their criticisms and proposals are not about policy. Cavalier argues that "the central problem with the Labor Party is that it is controlled lock, stock and barrel by trade unions. 100 per cent of management power is in the hands of union leaders – not workers or unionists – and their "clients", the state general secretaries and the ruling and opposition factions.[234] He allows that until the late 1970s, the unions could mount a credible argument for their dominance within the ALP, based on their coverage of approximately 50 per cent of the Australian workforce. But by 2006 "fewer than 23 out of 100 … workers belong[ed] to unions, and fewer than 1 in 10 belong[ed] to unions affiliated to the ALP".[235] They enjoyed a fillip owing to their successful media campaign attacking the Howard Government's *Work Choices* legislation, but by 2008 they were suffering a further across the board decline.[236] So "[w]e're talking about the deliberate exclusion from the managing governance of the Party of about 92% of Australians".[237]

This catastrophic fall in affiliated union membership has not been "matched by any corresponding shift in the formal governance of the

---

[234] Rodney Cavalier, interview by James. Carleton2006.
[235] "Labor in Crisis."
[236] Cavalier, *Power Crisis: The Self-destruction of a State Labor Party*, p 53.
[237] "Labor in Crisis."

ALP. The Party failed to address the anachronism that unions without a social base remained in control of the ALP." [238] Because while ever senior affiliated union officials delivered for the parliamentary leaders, the un-representative character of the Party was a benefit to Labor governments, not a hindrance. "Electoral success was the elixir that sustained the denial of internal Party democracy."[239]

Cavalier explains how the key to the unions' power is control of the ALP's state conferences. Big blocs versus clusters of smaller ones means the former prevail. In the ALP, whether the ratio of union to non-union delegates is 60:40 or 30:70 it amounts to union control of the conference floor. "The ratio has to go below 20 before the bloc votes of unions cease to prevail", otherwise it translates into control of the conference agenda, proceedings and "atmospherics". It means winning the positions elected by conference, most importantly the Party's officers, the executive and delegates to national conference. It means control of the Party between conferences, and a dominant position at the following conference.[240] It is obvious to Cavalier that "[t]here cannot and will not be reform of the ALP until and unless legislation compels plebiscites on [unions'] affiliation to the Labor Party".[241] He also wants Labor to adopt a UK Labour style opting in/out rule for union members. Thus if the plebiscite led to a union's affiliation to the Labor Party, an individual could opt for their membership not to be counted for the purposes of the number of members the union affiliates to the ALP with. Cavalier also proposes that, in order to qualify for public funding of election campaigns, political parties must have democratic constitutions that vests control

---

[238] *Power Crisis: The Self-destruction of a State Labor Party*, p 33.

[239] Ibid.

[240] Ibid., p 31.

[241] Anna Patty, "John Faulkner's preselection proposal faces defeat," *Illawarra Mercury*, 18 July 2014.

in their membership.[242]

Faulkner says that the unions continue to be important for Labor, but that they are a declining "social force". Further, they are "large, faceless institutions controlled by union secretaries, who are in turn obedient to factional cartels."[243] Unionists have no direct say in their union's decisions within the ALP, its factional alignment or how it votes on preselections and policy. Their views are "filtered through layers of delegation" – their union's secretary.[244]

Faulkner proposes four major changes to the Labor Party's rules, and another to the law, so as to redress what he sees as the union secretaries' usurpation of power within the ALP.

- a 60-20-20 rule – 60 per cent of delegates to the Party's state conferences to be directly elected by the membership, 20 per cent by federal and state electorate councils and 20 per cent by affiliated trade unions;[245]

- ballots of union members to directly elect unions' delegates to state conferences;

- ballots of Party members to preselect candidates for state upper houses and the Senate;

- community preselections of candidates for state lower houses and the House of Representatives, with equal weighting of votes for Party members and "declared" Labor supporters; and

The above proposal for community preselections clearly reflects Faulkner's opinion of the Party's membership (he argues that branch attendance is "no longer the only way to measure activism and

---

[242] Rodney Cavalier, "Submission ot the Panel of Experts - Political Donations," (2014).

[243] John Faulkner, "Public Pessimism, Political Complacency: Restoring Trust, Reforming Labor," in *The Light on the Hill Society* (2014), p 14.

[244] Ibid.

[245] Faulkner suggests that this rule be introduced in stages, over the next three national conferences.

commitment", and so "voting in our internal ballots ought not to be regarded as a reward earned only by those able to negotiate arcane rules"[246]) and the esteem in which he holds "[p]rogressive, socially aware activists passionate about social and economic reform", who Faulkner says "must never be outsiders to the Labor movement".[247]

- for political parties to be eligible for public funding, their rules and decisions be made subject to judicial review.[248]

Faulkner's 60-20-20 rule would dramatically reduce the size of affiliated unions' delegations while increasing the number of member delegates from zero to a majority. Direct election of union members would put paid to senior union officials appointing their union's delegates. These two rule changes would effectively end the cartel of powerful union officials' and factional power brokers' stranglehold over state conferences (i.e. they would take out of senior union officials' hands their ability to deliver to factional power brokers large numbers of delegates' votes sufficient to pass or defeat any motion put at state conference), transferring it to the membership. Changing the rules so members directly vote in state-wide ballots for their upper houses and the Senate would remove a major source of patronage from the hands of the power brokers. Making political parties' rules and decisions[249] justiciable would make power brokers legally accountable for any attempt(s) to subvert the existing or new rules.

Federal parliamentarians on the right are sceptical of calls to further reduce the unions' role within the Party. Ed Husic, the Shadow

---

[246] Faulkner, "Public Pessism, Political Complacency, Restoring Trust, Reforming Labor."

[247] "Cultural reform essential for Labor," *The Australian*, 10 June 2011.

[248] Under current law, the courts have no jurisdiction in these internal affairs of political parties.

[249] Under the ALP's rules, delegates to state conference elect key committees, including the powerful administrative committee and public office selection committee, that play a major role in preselecting candidates. There are also appeal tribunals.

Minister for Employment Services and Workplace Participation, sees value in balancing the say of members and that of the unions, "given the historical connection we have had with unions within the Party"[250] since 1916. Moreover, according to the Shadow Minister for Defence, Richard Marles, the "influence of unions in ... the decision-making of the federal parliamentary Labor Party is vastly overstated."[251]

But senior union officials are the most outspoken critics of further watering down the unions' representation at state conferences. They include Ayers; Tony Sheldon, the National Secretary of the TWU; and Joe de Bruyn. Ayers and Sheldon are NSW factional leaders. Sheldon is a former senior vice president and member of the national executive. Ayers is a current, and de Bruyn a former, member of the national executive. Ayers claims that Faulkner "tinkers" with one element of the Party's structure, which is neither necessary nor sufficient to deal with the challenges facing the labour movement. Efforts to reform Labor must be rooted in strengthening the labour movement. Labor is strongest when the political and industrial wings work together.[252] Sheldon claims that under Faulkner's proposal the factions would continue if union representation were reduced from 50 to 20 per cent, but with power concentrated in fewer hands.[253] He opposes direct election for upper-house seats, but supports "rank-and-file ballots for parliamentary leaders and members of parliament.[254]

Arguably the clearest indication of the unions' resolve to hold on to their power was the action taken on 12 March 2015 by 15 senior

---

[250] Brad Norington and Sid Maher, "Union boss Tony Sheldon rejects call to cut party power," *The Australian*, 9 October 2014.

[251] Ibid.

[252] Tim Ayers, "5 Reasons Why Direct Action Isn't Good Enough," (2014). He instances the Your Rights at Work campaign in 20017.

[253] Norington and Maher, "Union boss Tony Sheldon rejects call to cut party power."

[254] Hannan, Ewan. "ALP reforms mere distraction, says TWU boss Tony Sheldon." *The Australian*, 25 April 2014.

union officials from the left and right in response to the maiden speech in the NSW LA by the member for Kogarah, Chris Minns, who said:

> Trade unions are integral to both our success and our heritage but Labor also needs to represent those who are not in a trade union. That will mean taking steps to reduce union control on the floor of our conference and increasing the representation of ordinary members of our Party to have more diverse voices echoing through the halls of this 124-year-old institution. Exceptional trade unionists fight every day for working people but sometimes – particularly at the conclusion of Labor's last term in office – they are shackled by an association within our tribe. In the long term a more balanced split in the make-up of Labor will be better both for the Party and for our hardworking trade unions.[255]

The union officials thereupon circulated an open letter to all ALP members of the NSW parliament accusing Minns of at best "naivety".[256] They argued, first, unions are the voice of working people, whether they are union members or not. Second, social democratic parties that seek to exclude or limit the role of unions end up unelectable as "a green left fringe group or a 'conservative lite' rump that stands for nothing other than to achieve power."[257] Minns, in his late 30s, was seen by many observers as a future leader of centre unity in NSW.[258]

For Cavalier like Oakes, reform creates losers, "officials of that sliver of trade unions that are affiliated to the ALP. Fewer than

[255] *Hansard*

[256] *Open letter to NSW ALP MPs regarding the maiden speech of the member of the member for Kogarah.*

[257] *Open letter to NSW ALP MPs regarding the maiden speech of the member of the member for Kogarah.*

[258] Following the resignation of Luke Foley in 2018, Minns made a bid for the NSW parliamentary leadership, and although unsuccessful he polled respectably in the open Caucus ballot.

50 individuals across Australia". Ever since 1916 the unions have imposed an "all-pervasive culture" of pre-conference caucuses and caucuses within caucuses. It is a "spoils" culture,[259] in which the purpose of organisation is self-advancement. Unions of the right and left have fought fierce ideological battles in decades past, but they always agreed unions should control the Party. Having agreed on this principle of Party organisation when divided by ideology, the heirs to the factional "labels" are unlikely to consent to reforming the basis of their control now that ideology is a thing of the past.[260]

But questionable though their motives may be, the 13 senior right and left wing NSW union officials who rebuked Minns over his comments on their dominance within the Party demonstrated their resolve to oppose any proposals to further reduce their representation at the NSW state conference. Moreover, Joe de Bruyn argues that Faulkner's proposed further reductions in unions' representation at state conferences are a ploy aimed at delivering the Party to the left.[261] Given the results from member elections of the Party president and the federal parliamentary leader, his concerns are well founded. Further, under Faulkner's community pre-selections stacking a pre-selection ballot would be made easier by people no longer required to join the Party in order to vote; they would only need to "declare" their support for Labor. The capture of UK Labour in 2015 shows how easy it is for a well organised minority on the far left to enrol members solely for this purpose.[262] One such

---

[259] The spoils currently shared among the factions include seats in upper houses and the Senate, and the positions of Party General Secretary, two assistant general secretaries and two organisers.

[260] Cavalier, *Power Crisis: The Self-destruction of a State Labor Party*, pp 31-32.

[261] Troy Bramston, "Defeat sparks call for ALP branch overhaul," *The Australian*, 12 April 2014.

[262] Janet Daley, "Corbyn's win a bad omen for a once-vital progressive party," *National Post*, 14 September 2015.

organisation already exists in Australia, with GetUp! reported by the 2010 Review as having 350,000 members in 2010; it also stated that in the same year the Party's national membership stood at approximately 45,000. Of a like mind to de Bruyn, Easson wrote that "a membership decides-all approach at present would deliver the ALP to the Left. The Left sees its chance."[263]

Fading membership[264]

The academic suggestion for a more "diverse" membership did not address the dramatic decline in formal Party membership. Cavalier's contention that an unrepresentative structure was the main cause of the decline in the Party's membership and branch structure is unconvincing. The more persuasive suggestion by Katz attributes the decline in the Party's membership to broader societal change, unrelated to party structure. Australian scholars applied theories of gradual political party change developed by their Western European colleagues to changes that have taken place within the ALP in response changes in Australia's economic and social conditions over the post-war period. The theories include the "electoral professional" model suggested by Angelo Panebianco and the "cartel" theory developed by Richard Katz and Peter Mair. The Australian academic who did the most work in applying these theories locally were Ian Ward, Stephen Mills and Ian Marsh.

In Panebianco's electoral professional model,[265] the importance of membership diminishes, so, too, do ties with the social class whence the parties sprang. Ideology is replaced by "issues", and true believers by "interest groups". Parties come to rely on professionals,

---

[263] Easson, "The Right approach for a tired organisation."

[264] Adapted from the title of Andrew Scott's book *Fading Loyalties*

[265] Angelo Panebianco, *Political Parties: Organization and Power* (Cambridge, England: Cambridge University Press, 1988).

who take over from old style operatives, especially market researchers and pollsters to conduct election campaigns. Parties are forced to seek public funding to cover these professional costs. Less emphasis is placed on collective, internal leadership, with leadership becoming more personalised. The move towards this model is driven in part by changing social stratification, which altered the major political parties' original constituencies, thereby weakening party identification. But also by unprecedented development in communications, in particular the advent of television. Applying electoral professional theory to Australia, Ian Ward found that the ALP's traditional working class base was eroding, and its branch structure appeared to be in jeopardy. It relied upon public funding and donations from outside the labour movement. Moreover, the Party was staffed by market researchers and other policy advisers with specialist skills not found within the Party, and these professionals were shaping Labor's election campaigns. Further, in an age of presidential style politics, greater emphasis was being placed upon Labor leaders, giving them ever more say in shaping Party policy. For Ward, the electoral professional theory appeared to make sense of changes the ALP was undergoing at the outset of the 21st century.[266]

The term cartel refers to a commercial practice having a lineage in economic theory and legal principle. Proponents of the cartel model say the concept can be applied to contemporary political practices. They argue that, although competing against each other, major parties act in concert to "monopolise" political office; their cartel-like practices ensure them privileged access to public resources,

---

[266] Ian Ward, "Cartel parties and election campaigns in Australia," in *Political Parties in Transition*, ed. Ian. Marsh (Leichhardt, NSW: The Federation Press, 2006), pp 80-81.

which they use to consolidate their positions and deter entrants.[267] Katz and Mair[268] first emphasised the extent to which today's political parties rely on government subsidies. They argued that major parties are able to exploit their "role as governors and law-makers" to secure financial support from the state, which allows them to "flourish in the face of declining membership and dissipating voter loyalties".[269]

Bramble and Kuhn found that the forms of state funding in Australia include "direct grants by state and federal governments to cover election costs ... Other subsidies include public funding of party-aligned research centres (initiated by the Keating Government) and international activities, tax deductions for donations to the Party [including tax deductions on parliamentary levies[270]], and free election broadcasts on ABC and SBS television and radio";[271] political parties "also receive state funding *indirectly* through parliamentarians' salaries and allowances".[272] Botterill and Fenna also point out that, because Australian government payments to cover election costs are based on past election results, incumbent political parties can build up their monetary resources in order to resist any challengers, effectively entrenching the power of the major parties and raising barriers to new entrants.[273] Nicole Bolleyer and Gauja sought insight into the

---

[267] Botterill and Fenna argue that, while public funding has a democratic rationale, it may serve undemocratic ends if it is not equally available to new parties. (Linda Botterill and Alan Fenna, "Political parties and the party system," in *Government and Politics in Australia*, ed. Alan. Fenna, Jane. Robbins, and John. Summers (Frenchs Forest: Pearson, 2014), p 143.)

[268] Katz and Mair, "Changing Models of Party Organization and Party Democracy: The Emergence of the Cartel Party."

[269] Ibid., p 15.

[270] A rarely mentioned source of funding for the ALP is the substantial levies imposed on its parliamentary members.

[271] Bramble and Kuhn, "Continuity or Discontinuity in the Recent History of the Australian Labor Party?," p 288.

[272] Ibid.

[273] Botterill and Fenna, "Political parties and the party system," p 143.

leeway that Australian political parties have "to intensify incumbency advantages and therefore distort fair competition".[274] Bolleyer and Gauja found that, "despite varying regulatory regimes applicable to the various parliamentary resources, both monetary and non-monetary resources[275] were capable of exploitation".[276]

Mills argued that Australia's public funding arrangements suggest a "compelling case of cartel-like behaviour" between the Labor Party and the Liberal Party.

> It is not a perfectly exclusive cartel: minor parties are eligible to share taxpayers' bounty when their first preference vote exceeds 4 per cent. Even so, the lion's share of the funding goes to the two major parties and they remain the dominant players as a result: public funding allows them to engage the largest teams of professionals and to mount the most expensive professional campaigns, thereby retaining their parliamentary majorities and remaining the principal cartel members.[277]

Similarly, Bramble and Kuhn were of the view that the ALP had undergone changes in the second half of the twentieth century, "as the 'cartel Party' proponents emphasise".[278] But that "[a] variety of indicators confirm that Labor's [firm base in society] still rests predominantly in the working class".[279]

However, rather than access to public resources, Blyth and Katz

---

[274] Nicole Bolleyer and Anika Gauja, "The Limits of Regulation: Indirect Party Access to State Resources in Australia and the United Kingdom," *Governance: An International Journal of Policy, Administration and Insititutions* 28, no. 3 (2015): p 321.

[275] Bolleyer and Gauja distinguish monetary from nonmonetary public resources. They reported on research showing the monetary value of "in kind" resources (support services such as phones, computers, mailing lists, printing and the like) in Australia "constitutes between 50% and 70% of total Party income – a significant source when compared to donations, direct state funding and membership fees". Ibid., p 323.

[276] Ibid., p 334.

[277] Mills, *The Professionals: Strategy, Money and the Rise of the Political Campaigner*, p 281.

[278] Bramble and Kuhn, "Continuity or Discontinuity in the Recent History of the Australian Labor Party?," p 292.

[279] Ibid., p 285.

identify ideological convergence as the defining characteristic of the cartel model. Major political parties adopt similar approaches to public policy. This bipartisanship has the effect of limiting opportunities for voters to express their dissatisfaction with such policies, and the established parties can discredit as irresponsible alternative policies championed by new and minor parties. Ian Marsh claims that convergence is a response among economists and commentators to a set of external, often independent, economic, cultural and other forces broadly described as "globalisation", of which the economic was the most significant.[280] Marsh found that there began a convergence of economic policy positions between Labor and the Coalition around the free market and internationalisation of the Australian economy. These "neo-liberal" policies were "progressively introduced with broad bipartisan support following the election of the Hawke Government in 1983".[281]

Taken together Ward's, Mill's, Marsh's and other academics' findings suggest that, at least from the early 1980's, the Party has attempted to construct an electoral bulwark against the weakening in party identification noted by the 2002 Review, and the dramatic decline in its membership and branch structure bemoaned by the 2010 Review. This "strategy" includes the Party's reliance on market researchers and pollsters for its campaigns, on private donations from outside the labour movement,[282] on Labor's tacit collusion with the Liberal Party for the purpose of corralling the lion's share of taxpayers' largesse, and emphasis on personalised leadership (most notably the parliamentary

---

[280] For a contrary view see Murray Goot, "Party Convergence Reconsidered," ibid.39, no. 1 (2004).

[281] Ian Marsh, "Australia's political cartel?," in *Political Parties in Transition?*, ed. Ian. Marsh (Annandale, NSW: The Federation Press, 2006), pp 6-7. Marsh claimed they revolutionised Australia's "strategic socio-economic agenda".

[282] Of course, unions (often including unaffiliated unions) provide Labor with crucial support during elections – financial and volunteers to work polling booths.

leadership of Bob Hawke). As well, Labor and the Liberal Party have at times limited their policy differences, such as over immigration intake levels and the Hawke Government's economic reforms, which has effectively limited voters' ability to register their disaffection with the major parties at election time.

5

THE REVIEWS' CONSEQUENCES FOR LABOR POLICY

Marian Sawer argued that the 1979 Inquiry was guilty of a "blame the victim" theme – women and minorities.[283] On the contrary wrote Johns, the 1979 Inquiry predicted the aggressive agendas of the organised special interest groups, the so-called "minorities". [284] The Victorian ALP Secretary, Bob Hogg, in his *Draft Report to the Sub-Committee of the ALP National Committee of Inquiry*, stated that the Party's policy was determined by the articulate, educated, middle-class, and that it had lost touch with the views and aspirations of its working-class supporters.[285]

---

[283] Marian Sawer, "A defeat for political correctness?," in *The Politics of Retribution: The 1996 Australian Federal Election*, ed. Clive Bean (St. Leonards, NSW: Allen & Unwin, 1997), p 79.

[284] Gary Johns, 1997, 'Whither Labor', *Backgrounder* Vol. 9/2. p. 3, Institute of Public Affairs.

[285] Quoted in Andrew Scott, *Fading loyalties: The Australian Labor Party and the Working Class* (Leichhardt, NSW: Pluto Press, 1991), pp 24-5.

This chapter, first, briefly details the "encouragement" given by Labor to those the 1979 Inquiry called "neglected elements". Second, it looks at whether others may be feeling disaffected by Labor's policy of encouragement, and suggests policies it should adopt to allay their grievances. Third, and relatedly, it looks at why the working class now see themselves as Labor's "forgotten people", and how it might go-about retaining or regaining their loyalty.

"Neglected elements"

As discussed above, since the 1979 Inquiry women's participation has been encouraged by means of affirmative action, such that by 2025 50 per cent of Labor parliamentarians must be women. This policy is the only recommendation pursued unremittingly by the Reviews. From the Wyndham Plan onwards, Australia's youth has also been encouraged by the ALP;[286] AYL now sends three delegates to the Party's 400 delegate national conference.[287]

The Reviews have also sought to encourage those of ethnic origin to join the Party. The 1979 Inquiry made a series of recommendations,[288] including establishing ethnic branches at which the meetings would be conducted in the community language (this recommendation was adopted by Victoria, although not by NSW), but none have gone so far as to make recommendations for affirmative action or delegates to national conference. Rather, "[t]he Party has provided an avenue for ethnic activists wishing to pursue a political career. Such activists can use their ethnic community base

---

[286] Wyndham, "Australian Labor Party Reorganisation: Recommendations of the General Secretary " p 15. Recommendation 21.

[287] ALP, "National Platform 2015," (2015), p 8.

[288] Bill Hayden and Bob Hawke, "National Committee of Inquiry: Report and Recommendations to the National Executive," (Australian Labor Party, 1979), p 14. Recommendation H5

to help in their endeavour. They have made significant inroads as Party functionaries and representatives."[289] Or as Lyle Allan puts it, the encouragement given ethnic communities was by way of "branch stacking". And if not all branch stacking is ethnically or religiously based, it is the most successful.[290]

Just on 75 per cent of Lebanese Muslims in Australia had settled in Sydney's south western suburbs (initially in Lakemba and Auburn) by 2011.[291] The Muslim percentage of the population in the federal electorates of Watson (which includes the suburb of Lakemba) and Blaxland (which includes part of Auburn) are 22.0 and 27.1 per cent, respectively[292] (the seat of Blaxland is held by Jason Clare and Watson by Tony Burke, both are centre unity faction shadow frontbenchers). This influx has led to lobbying for political representation, with a number of individuals from the Lebanese Muslim community gaining Party preselection and successfully campaigning for political office as Labor candidates, mostly in local government but also in the NSW Parliament. Shaoquette Moselmane entered the LC in 2009, and was subsequently elected Opposition Whip; Jihad Dib was elected to the LA in 2015, and has since been

---

[289] Bob Birrell, Ernest Healy, and Lyle Allan, "Labor's Shrinking Constituency," *People and Place* 13, no. 2 (2005): p 52.

[290] Lyle Allan, "Ethnic Recruitment or Ethnic Branch Stacking?: Factionalism and Ethnicity in the Victorian ALP," ibid.8, no. 1 (2000): p 29. But the courting of ethno-religious communities can be a double-edged sword, as Labor learned to its consternation. At the last NSW state election, the LMA criticised recently elected Opposition Leader Foley, and backed his Liberal opponent Ronny Oueik in the seat of Auburn, following Labor's decision not to preselect the LMA's controversial preferred candidate Hicham Zraika who had been suspended from the Labor Party for "unworthy conduct". LMA President Samier Dandan said Labor should have preselected Zraika, an Auburn councillor who "was well groomed to run for that seat" Nicole Hasham, "NSW election: Muslim group turns on Labor leader Luke Foley in Auburn," *The Sydney Morning Herald*, 26 March 2015.

[291] James Jupp, ed. *The Australian People: An Encyclopaedia of the Nation, Its Peoples and their Origin* (Cambridge, UK: Cambridge University Press, 2001), p 564.

[292] Percentages calculated from data in ABS (2016) *Commonwealth Electoral Divisions*.

promoted to Labor's spokesperson on education. Moselmane and Dib enjoyed strong backing from centre unity. John Robertson, during his tenure as Opposition Leader, had the preselection for the seat of Lakemba referred to the national executive, with the recommendation that Dib be endorsed as Labor's candidate for the seat,[293] while Richardson claimed[294] that "more than any other individual I am responsible for getting the Labor Party to put [Moselmane] into parliament. ... He was the first Muslim elected to the NSW parliament."[295]

The disaffected

In encouraging the neglected elements, others within the electorate, including some within these elements and others affected by them, may be feeling disaffected by what they see as the Party's preferential treatment of interest groups, and which may be affecting their support for Labor. Analysing the possible sources of the disaffected elements' grievances leads to brief suggestions for Labor on re-prioritising its policies so as to retain or win their electoral support.

"Women"

In his contribution to *Labor Essays 1982*, Ben Chifley's biographer, Fin Crisp, wrote:

---

[293] Sean. Nicholls, "Celebrated principal Jihad Dib to be parachuted in as ALP candidate despite John Robertson's democracy claim," *The Sydney Morning Herald*, 5 September 2014. Dib would not have won a community ballot.

[294] Although no longer a senior Party officer or parliamentarian, Richardson retains much of his influence within centre unity.

[295] Graham. Richardson, "Talk at lunch, not in court, over Israel," *The Australian* 4 March 2016.

[A]n ALP National Conference in 1981 fell for a proposal from essentially white-collar and professional-class feminists for the adoption of 'affirmative action' by way of assuring ALP women aspirants of the preselections for a set proportion of Labor's safer seats. … There are relatively few blue-collar women active in the branches taken as a whole and very few of those who could compete at preselection or election with white collar women who are joining the ALP branches and aspiring to parliamentary careers in significantly rising numbers. Seen in the light of these facts, the pre-empting of safe seats in substantially blue-collar areas for middle-class ALP women is a sure prescription for further weakening the steadily declining shares in ALP parliamentary, ministerial and leadership representation of the ALP blue collar base.[296]

Affirmative action works to benefit "white-collar and professional-class feminists" in that the recruitment of so-called "quality candidates" by the factions and sub-factions who typically apportion seats in federal and state parliaments invariably translates as university educated (for women and for men). Moreover, few women coming through the union movement are employed in routine white collar jobs in the services sector.

The 2002 Review's observation that Labor had failed to retain the support of women from lower socio-economic backgrounds suggests that Crisp's criticism of Labor's affirmative action for women policy fell on deaf ears. But Australia is not the only western country in which a left leaning political party has fallen for this sort of affirmative action proposal. In 2010 Owen Jones wrote that, laudable though UK Labour's goal of increasing the number of women candidates standing for parliament was, it "largely ended up

---

[296] L. F Crisp, "The Labor Party: Then and Now," in *Labor Essays 1982: Socialist Principles and Parliamentary Government*, ed. Gareth. Evans and John. Reeves (Richmond, Vic.: Drummond Publishing, 1982), pp 79-80.

promoting middle-class women with professional backgrounds rather than candidates sharing the backgrounds of millions of working-class women in low-paid, part-time, service-sector jobs."[297] Thomas Frank, author of *Listen Liberal*, writing about a Clinton Foundation event held on International Women's Day in 2015 observed that "[t]here was no consideration – I mean, zero – of the situation of women who work on the shop floors of the Fortune 500 ... or any of the countless low-wage employers who make that list sparkle. Working-class American women were simply ... not there. In this festival of inclusiveness and sweet affirmation, *their* problems were not considered, *their* voices were not heard."[298]

Verity Bergmann and Andrew Milner in 1996 had pointed out the self-interest within the Australian "women's movement", which "has more obviously espoused the concerns of educated professional women than those of more disadvantaged women."[299] They singled out the developing "femocracy [that, in practice,] has provided a stratum of women intellectuals with successful, well paid careers, whilst achieving much less to advantage the position of the majority of women".[300]

A year later, Belinda Prober cast doubt on the 1979 Inquiry claim of a move by women from a "predominantly domestic role" to the full-time paid workforce when she wrote that analysis of the census data by Gregory and Hunter:

> strongly suggest ... it is quite mistaken to see the traditional family

[297] Jones, *Chavs: The Demonisation of the Working Class*, pp 255-6.

[298] Thomas Frank, *Listen Liberal or Whatever Happened To The Party Of The People* (Melbourne: Scribe, 2016), pp 242-3.

[299] Verity Burgmann and Andrew Milner, "Intellectuals and the New Social Movements," in *Class and Class conflict in Australia*, ed. Rick. Kuhn and Tom. O'Lincoln (Melbourne, Vic.: Longman, 1996), pp 123-24.

[300] Ibid., p 123.

form as dying out in the face of contemporary ideologies of women's emancipation and growing employment opportunities for women. They have shown that the pattern of employment change for women between 1976 and 1991 is radically different for high socio-economic status neighbourhoods than for low socio-economic status neighbourhoods. For the top half of neighbourhoods the proportion of women employed increased approximately 10 per cent. For the bottom half of neighbourhood's employment fell by 40 per cent.[301]

Moreover, Prober found that, in the poorer working class single income families, "[c]hildren were the central focus of these women's lives and of their identities – and were also the main source of pleasure in their lives ... getting a job was seen as extremely difficult and unattractive."[302] These women are critical of parenting allowances; they "strongly preferred ... decent wages for their [husbands] and the lump sum payment that had come with the old dependent-spouse rebate".[303]

Writing in 1998, Bettina Arndt also cast doubt on the 1979 Inquiry's claim, quoting Bob Gregory as saying that a "really big story" is that "[a]ll the growth in employment of women that occurred over the previous three decades basically stopped in the '90s".[304] Arndt wrote that:

> "[c]ontrary to popular assumptions, there have long been signs that women were resisting the lure of the working wage. For the past 30 years it has become obvious that the commitment most women

---

[301] Belinda Probert, "Gender and Choice: The Structure of Opportunity," in *Work of the Future: Global Perspectives*, ed. Paul. James, Walter. Veit, and Steve. Wright (St Leonards, NSW: Allen & Unwin, 1997), p 159.

[302] For some of these women, their choice may have been influenced in part by access to and the cost of child care relative to potential earnings from paid work.

[303] Probert, "Gender and Choice: The Structure of Opportunity," p 190.

[304] Bettina. Arndt, *The Sydney Morning Herald* 21 April 1998.

still show towards raising their families is putting a steady brake on their paid work. ... So there appears to be a distinct element of *choice* in women's involvement in part-time work [italics added]."[305]

In research conducted for the AIFS in 1997, Helen Glezer and Ilene Wolcott had found that of the mothers who work part-time, 70 per cent were happy with these hours, and 50 per cent of women working full-time would prefer to work shorter hours.[306] Almost a decade after Glezer's and Wolcott's report was published; the AIFS's Lixia Qu and Ruth Weston took a fresh look at "whether mothers' preferences changed during this time". They concluded that Glezer's and Wolcott's finding that "most mothers whose youngest child is aged under five years or five to twelve years want some paid work (preferably part-time) and that roughly half of those who were working full-time want to work 'shorter hours' ... appeared to hold in 2003."[307] Importantly, Qu and Weston noted that some mothers "may" want to enter the paid workforce or increase their current hours because doing so is the lesser of two evils, "the other being exposing their family to financial difficulties", which would describe the situation faced by most "disadvantaged women".[308]

In *Labor without class: The gentrification of the ALP*, my questioning of the 1979 Inquiry's recommendations for women drew on the foregoing research (all except Qu's and Weston's). In *Party Girls:*

---

[305] Ibid.
[306] Helen Glezer and Ilene Wolcott, "Work and family values, preferences and practice," 4 (1997).
[307] Lixia Qu and Ruth Weston, "A woman's place? Work hour preferences revisited: nearly a decade has elapsed since the report by Glezer and Wolcott on mothers' work hours preferences. Lixia Qu and Ruth Weston look at whether mothers' preferences changed during this time," *Family Matters*, no. 72 (2005): p 76.
[308] Ibid., pp 76-7.

Labor Women Now,[309] which was released in the following year, several feminist contributors were dismissive of my arguments – however, they chose not to respond to the research I drew on.

In its 2017 employment study of Australia, the OECD was reported as claiming "[t]here are potentially large losses to the economy when women *stay at home* or work shorter part-time hours [italics added]". For these women themselves there are personal losses, as "paid work" is "important for women's personal wellbeing and perceptions of their overall quality of life".[310]

If, as the 1979 Inquiry argued, Labor's real concern with women is for "electoral purposes", it is suggested that, to win the support of women from low-socio-economic backgrounds, "choice" of a career, part-time work or homemaking should all, equally, be the focus of Labor's policies for women – with no smearing of part-time women workers and homemakers as a drain on the economy and unfulfilled, nor further use of the pejorative term "stay at homes".

Older Australians

AYL is now little more than a training ground for operatives (most of whom are graduates from student politics), many of them aspiring parliamentarians. Its members no longer represent the interests of the multitude of young people not directly engaged in politics.

In an essay for the Evatt Foundation in 2005,[311] Encel told of the NSW Branch's inquiry that "matched" the 2002 Review, one of whose recommendations was for the "appointment of a 'task force'

---

[309] Kate Deverall et al., eds., *Party Girls: Labor Women Now* (Annandale, NSW: Pluto Press, 2000).

[310] Natasha Bita, "Mums: You are a waste stuck at home," *The Daily Telegraph* 10 March 2017.

[311] Encel, "Labor and the Future: Where to now?."

on demographic change" for the purpose of analysing the decline in Labor's primary vote. The task force (of which Encel was a member) pointed out the "anomaly of a situation where 75 per cent of people over 65 are pensioners, but only one-third of them are likely to vote Labor".[312] Given the "rapid growth of the older population, this should be a priority for the ALP". The task force's report was presented to the 2003 NSW Conference, but "received virtually no discussion, and [was not] distributed to the Party branches".[313]

Encel's priority was not shared by the 2010 Review; rather, it bemoaned the ageing of the Party's membership, as if its authors were unaware (although presumably they were) that Australia's rapidly ageing population would be reflected in the Party's membership. Indeed, they were dismayed the ageing of the Party's membership was becoming more severe.[314]

By turning its back on older Australians, the Party is depriving Labor of their votes. It is suggested, therefore, that the Party start listening to pensioners – particularly those who are asset poor. It could begin by establishing Australian Senior Labor (analogous to AYL), including sending delegates to national conference so as to represent the interests of older Australians. Labor's platform provides that: "Every state Administrative Committee or state Executive should consider co-opting a non-voting member or members of Young Labor."[315] If the Party establishes Australian Senior Labor, it should similarly provide for its membership.

---

[312] Ibid.

[313] Ibid.

[314] Bracks, Faulkner, and Carr, "2010 National Review: Report to the ALP National Executive," p 10. Cross and Gauja went further than the 2010 Review, claiming that those who are members of the Party tend to be older and, "generally unrepresentative of Australian society". Cross and Gauja, "Evolving membership strategies in Australian political parties," p 614.

[315] ALP, "Labor National Platform A Fair Go For Australia," (ALP, 2018), p 303.

"From the [western] suburbs"[316]

Seamus O'Hanlon and Rachel Stevens noted that multiculturalism and immigration "was and is an overwhelming urban ... phenomenon".[317] In Sydney, "gentrification since the 1970s increasingly meant that newer immigrants tended to settle in outer suburbs".[318] By 1991, "the effects of nearly two decades of non-discriminatory immigration policies were visibly apparent in Australian major cities, especially Sydney"[319] with its greater ethnic diversity.[320]

The following analysis looks at how the actual experience with multiculturalism and immigration policies have shaped the attitudes of the working class residents in outer western Sydney, with the evidence suggesting that many of them do not accept the elite's and governments' prevailing orthodoxy on either of these policies (and related cultural issues).

Consultants to the 1989 Fitzgerald Report, the most influential report on Australia's immigration policy, found that "not only Anglo-Celtic Australians but also immigrants of many years standing are 'very angry' about multicultural policy".[321] In 1994, John Hirst considered the attitudes of "ordinary people" to multiculturalism, and argued that it "met a good deal of popular resistance. But there was also a measure of acceptance – of the multicultural rather than of

---

[316] From the suburbs Dave Warner 1978
[317] Seamus O'Hanlon and Rachel Stevens, "A Nation of Immigrants or a Nation of Immigrant Cities? The Urban Context of Australian Multiculturalism," *Australian Journal of Political Science* 63, no. 4 (2017): p 560.
[318] Ibid., p 567.
[319] Ibid., p 565.
[320] Ibid., p 566.
[321] Stephen Fitzgerald, "Immigration - A commitment to Australia," (Canberra: Australian Government Publishing Service, 1989), pp 30-1.

multiculturalism".[322] Ordinary people, Hirst wrote, "had no awareness of the *agenda* which lay behind the term [italics added]. They took it to be a new expert word descriptive of Australian society and of the attitudes which they have long displayed towards migrants: tolerance and a satisfaction in seeing migrants participate in Australian life."[323]

The 2011 Mapping Social Cohesion survey found that 72 per cent of Coalition voters and 60 per cent of Labor voters thought it better if migrants "adapt and blend in" to Australian society, rather than government assisting them to maintain their customs and traditions.[324] The 2017 Mapping Social Cohesion survey found that 58 per cent of respondents to its 2016 survey disagreed with the proposition that governments should provide assistance to ethnic minorities to enable them to "maintain their customs and traditions", with only 34 per cent in agreement.[325] Even absent the provision of government assistance, Andrew Markus noted that when two polls conducted in 1992 and 1993 posed the proposition that "'Immigrants to this country should be prepared to adopt *the way of life of this country*'" there was a very high level of agreement, 87 per cent in the first poll and 86 per cent in the second; 13 per cent and 14 per cent respectively were in disagreement

---

[322] The Minister for Immigration and Ethnic Affairs in the Hawke Government, Chris Hurford, stressed the significance of this distinction when he wrote: Alas, some, particularly in the academic class, have gone over the top and converted the adjective multicultural into a noun, multiculturalism. They have left the impression that separate development of these cultures should be an objective of policy ... This has never been the objective of our policy, nor should it be. We are not, nor should we be, a nation of many cultures. We are a multicultural nation that strongly celebrates core Western cultural values of liberal democracy. (Chris Hurford, "Chris Hurford: Silver lining to Hilali," *The Australian*, 2 November 2006.)

[323] John. Hirst, "National Pride and Multiculturalism," *People and Place* 2, no. 3: p 2.

[324] Andrew Markus, "Not prejudiced on asylum issue," *The Australian*, 27 September 2011.

[325] "Mapping Social Cohesion: The Scanlon Foundation Survey 2017 " (2017), p 67.

[italics added]."[326] However, in 2006 the ECCV charged that "claims to an *Australian way of life* are both nebulous and highly contested [italics added]".[327] Still, the 2011 Mapping Social Cohesion survey found that an overwhelming majority of respondents, 70 per cent of Coalition voters and 62 per cent of Labor voters, strongly agreeing it is important to maintain "an Australian way of life".[328] The 2017 Mapping Social Cohesion survey reported that the 2016-17 Scanlon Foundation surveys found that "close to two out of three respondents (in the range of 60%-66%) agreed with the proposition people who come to this country should "change their behaviour to be more like Australians".[329]

The 2017 Mapping Social Cohesion survey claimed that there has been "considerable volatility" in public attitudes towards immigration over the past 30 years.[330] In the early 1990s, a large majority (70% at its peak) considered the intake level to be too high, whereas this has been a minority view in "most" surveys conducted since 2000. Two contemporary surveys that do not figure among the "most" surveys are the 2016 Statement about immigration survey, which found that 59 per cent of those surveyed thought "[t]he level of immigration into Australia over the last ten years has been

---

[326] "Attitudes To Multiculturalism and Cultural Diversity," in *Multiculturalism and Integration: a Harmonious Relationship*, ed. James. Jupp and Michael. Clyne (Canberra, ACT: ANU Press, 2011), p 95. Markus had noted previously that, "[w]hen in 1988 respondents were asked whether 'people who come to Australia should change their behaviour to be more like other Australians', a clear majority, 66 per cent, were in agreement."

[327] Ethnic Communities' Council of Victoria, "Submission to the Discussion Paper, Australian Citizenship: Much more than a ceremony," (2006).

[328] Markus, "Not prejudiced on asylum issue."

[329] "Mapping Social Cohesion: The Scanlon Foundation Survey 2017 " p 67. It also found that the same percentage of respondents agreed with the proposition that "we should do more to learn about the customs and heritage of different ethnic and cultural groups in this country".

[330] Ibid., p 46.

too high",[331] while TAPRI's 2017 Research Report found that "74 per cent of voters believe that Australia does not need more people and that ... 54 per cent wanted a reduction in migrant intake".[332] Moreover, "[m]ost voters were also worried about the consequences of growing ethnic diversity."[333] The Lowy Institute's 2018 Poll found that a "majority (54%) say 'the total number of migrants coming to Australia each year is too high' ... [while] 41% say 'if Australia is too open to people from all over the world, we risk losing our identity as a nation'."[334]

Bob Birrell and Byong-Soo Seol highlighted the "growing concentration of low-income families in Sydney's south-west", who are primarily derived from NESB countries; "[t]hese recent arrivers are mainly locating in existing areas of high ethnic concentration."[335] They also found that the "concentrations identified are acute by any standard. ... [and] ... these concentrations are increasing."[336] Compounding these concentrations, in 2003 Ernest Healy and Birrell said their finding "raises the crucial issue of whether Australian-born residents are showing a relatively high propensity to move out of [western Sydney], thus accentuating the spatial concentration of low-income ethnic communities.[337] ... This possibility challenges those who argue that such concentrations would be relatively transitory (following the pattern of earlier post-war migrant groups) and not a

---

[331] Essential Media Communications, "Statement about immigration," *Essential Report* (2016).

[332] Katherine Betts and Bob Birrell, "Australian voters' views' on immigration policy," (The Australian Population Research Institute, 2017), p vi.

[333] Ibid., p v.

[334] Alex Oliver, Lowy Institute Poll 2018, p4.

[335] Bob Birrell and Byong-Soo Seol, "Sydney's Ethnic Underclass," *People and Place* 6, no. 3 (1998): p 25.

[336] Ibid., p 29.

[337] Ernest Healy and Bob Birrell, "Metropolis divided: The political dynamics of spatial inequality and migrant settlement in Sydney," ibid.11, no. 2 (2003): p 83.

more enduring feature of contemporary metropolitan development in Sydney."[338] Healy and Birrell's findings were supported by Bernard Salt who reported that:

> over the five years to 2016 ... up to two thirds of the 266,000 new arrivals in Sydney's western suburbs were not Australian-born and had a 'non-Anglo heritage'. ... Of those who departed over the same period, 63 per cent of the 183,000 total were Australian-born and a further 5 per cent were born in England or New Zealand.[339]

In January 2017, it was decided to settle "[a]t least half of Australia's special intake of 12,000 Syrian and Iraqi refugees ... in one part of western Sydney within 12 months"[340] – Fairfield. There is also the "'secondary settlement' phenomenon, with refugees moving to the Fairfield area after their initial arrival in other locations, some of which are interstate." [341] The ABC reported that "Fairfield ... is struggling to resettle refugees after a huge influx of new arrivals, mostly from Iraq and Syria."[342]

In June 2018, Brad Norrington wrote in *The Australian* that "[d]ebate over migrant enclaves was reignited last month when NSW Labor leader Luke Foley spoke out about 'white flight'[343] from [western] Sydney suburbs 'where many Anglo families have moved

---

[338] Ibid., p 69.
[339] Brad Norrington, "Complex truth of "white flight" revealed in data," *The Australian* 16 June 2018.
[340] Fergus Hunter, "Half of Australia's 12,000 Syrian and Iraqi refugees to be settled by just one Sydney council," *Sydney Morning Herald* 16 January 2017.
[341] Ibid.
[342] Penny Timms, "Fairfield struggles to cope after threefold increase in refugee arrivals", ABC News Online, 3 January 2017
[343] "Luke Foley was forced into a humiliating back down after federal and state Labor colleagues were furious he had injected race into the debate over immigration by using the contentious phrase 'white flight'". Anna Caldwell and Sharri Markson, "Sheer Foley," *The Daily Telegraph* 25 May 2018. The Refugee Council's Shakufa Tahiri was reported as saying "[w]hite flight is just a fancy term for racebaiting". Danielle Le Messurier, "Remark Raises Foley Hell," ibid.

out'."[344] Foley named Fairfield[345] as one of those suburbs with a "high concentration of Syrian and Iraqi refugees".[346]

The Mayor of Fairfield, Mr Frank Carbone, was reported as saying that, "[w]hile he disagreed with Mr Foley's use of language, the NSW Opposition Leader had raised valid issues. 'What's pushing people out is the strain on [services and infrastructure]', he said."[347] And then there is also the inflation in Sydney's house prices in recent decades.[348] Stephen Bali, President of the Western Sydney Regional Organisation of Councils and mayor of nearby Blacktown, was reported as raising local governments' responsibility for *social cohesion* [italics added]",[349] suggesting that this is also a factor. Mayor Carbone insisted: "Fairfield has done the heavy lifting for the nation" on Iraqi and Syrian refugees.[350]

Danielle Le Messurier in *The Daily Telegraph* reported on the views of three local residents:

> Assyrian Charlie Ukhanna, 75, has been a Fairfield resident for 38 years and agrees there has been a 'white flight' ... You used to go in the pub and there were all Aussies and now the pub is empty, nobody in there. ... I don't think they're coming back. Margo Connell has lived in the area for 60 years and has noticed the slow ebb of white Australia like her leaving the community. ... A few

[344] Norrington, "Complex truth of "white flight" revealed in data."
[345] The others suburbs were Guildford, Granville, Yennora and Regents Park, some fall with in his electorate of Auburn.
[346] Norrington, "Complex truth of "white flight" revealed in data."
[347] Ibid.
[348] Bob Birrell and Ernest Healy, "Immigration and the Housing Affordability Crisis in Sydney and Melbourne "*The Australian Population Research Institute* (July 2018): p v. Birrell and Healy partly attributed the, until recently, soaring Sydney house prices to immigration.
[349] Hunter, "Half of Australia's 12,000 Syrian and Iraqi refugees to be settled by just one Sydney council."
[350] Norrington, "Complex truth of "white flight" revealed in data."

of the older residents, we do feel like we're strangers in this area because of how much it's changed in such a short time, she said. It's not the same ... it's a completely different atmosphere to what it used to be when there were more Australians. Stewart Carson, 51, agreed with Mr Foley's 'white flight' comment. What he said he can't say by himself because people complain. But it's true, I never see Australian people here anymore, he said.[351]

Birrell was reported as saying "evidence proved Mr Foley was right about population movements in the western suburbs, even if his choice of phrase was politically unfortunate".[352] He went on to say, "just as arriving migrants found their living circumstances difficult, 'Anglo' locals experienced strains because sudden high concentrations of newcomers with non-English-speaking backgrounds and different cultures led to noticeable changes in the composition of schools,[353] clubs, civic associations and shopping areas. Residents often no longer recognised their suburb, and felt uncomfortable."[354] This prompts Anglo residents who can afford it to move out to more culturally sympathetic suburbs.

The related issue of integration into Australia society is as contentious as is the concentration of ethnic communities, particularly immigrants derived from Muslim countries. Data presented by Betts in 2002 showed that, while most respondents wanted either to accept more or to keep things as they are for British, Southern Europeans and Asians, a "majority (53 per cent) want[ed] Australia to accept

---

[351] Le Messurier, "Remark Raises Foley Hell."

[352] Norrington, "Complex truth of "white flight" revealed in data."

[353] Birrell said "[s]chools figure as a 'big' issue motivating departures ... A 60 to 70 per cent influx of migrants could greatly alter cultural concentrations in the classroom. 'Anglo' parents sought schools outside the area with more familiar settings."

[354] Norrington, "Complex truth of "white flight" revealed in data."

fewer immigrants from the Middle East".[355] For Betts, this introduced a new theme into Australian immigration politics. "Can Muslim immigrants from the Middle East be *integrated* in the same fashion as Orthodox Greeks or secular Chinese, or is the challenge qualitatively different [italics added]?"[356] While not forming part of a comparison with other faiths and ethnicities, almost a decade and a half later the Essential Media Report found that 41 per cent of respondents believed that Muslims "do not *integrate* into Australian society [italics added]."[357] As to the publics' opinion of Muslims more generally, the Scanlon Foundation's seven surveys (2010-12, 2014-17) found "a relatively high level of *negative opinion* towards Muslims, similar to the findings of the 2013 VicHealth survey. Over the course of its surveys, *negative opinion* has been in the range of 22%-25% (11%-14% very negative), at an average of 24%. This compares to 4%-5% *negative opinion* towards Christians (average 4.5%) and Buddhists (average 4.5%) [italics added]".[358] TAPRI's 2017 Research Report found that "[f]orty eight per cent supported a partial ban on Muslim immigration to Australia, with only 25 per cent in opposition".[359]

The threat of Muslim's committing terrorist acts was not a contributing factor to this "negative opinion" – according to Markus in 2017. The Scanlon Foundation surveys found that, "while concern over national security and the threat of terrorism has significantly increased there has been no statistically significant shift in the *negative opinion* towards Muslims over the course of the seven surveys [italics

---

[355] Katharine Betts, "Immigration and public opinion: understanding the shift," *People and Place* 10, no. 4 (2002): p 33.

[356] Ibid., pp 33-34.

[357] Essential Research, "The Essential Media Report,," (2 August 2016), p 6.

[358] Markus, "Mapping Social Cohesion: The Scanlon Foundation Survey 2017 " p 57.

[359] Betts and Birrell, "Australian voters' views' on immigration policy," p v.

added]".[360] The researcher Charles Miller reported on the findings of two studies of conflict between Muslim immigrants and natives in France[361] and the Netherlands[362] that "emphasised primarily *social value* differences as the key to *anti-Muslim sentiment* in Europe [italics added]"[363] – especially differences concerning women.

The 2013 Committee on Migration heard from Ms Heba Ibrahim, Assistant Secretary of the Executive Committee of AFIC, that "Islam does not support segregation of women, but *cultural or social etiquettes* in certain circumstances often do [italics added]".[364] One such is the arrangements to "accommodate" Muslim women at council run swimming pools, such as at Auburn.[365] Another form is the burka, which "is rarely worn in Australia, but many Islamic women choose to cover their faces with a veil known as the niqab, which covers all of

---

[360] Markus, "Mapping Social Cohesion: The Scanlon Foundation Survey 2017" p 57. However, writing early in the previous decade, Betts noted that the Australian Election Study her table was based on was held in the wake of: vicious gang rapes in Sydney perpetrated by youths of Lebanese origin from the Western suburbs" ... and "after the September 11 tragedy in the United States (largely engineered by Muslims from the Middle East). And after the Tampa incident, when the first boatload of asylum-seekers from the Middle East was prevented from disembarking on Australian territory. Many talkback radio callers in Australia in August 2001 linked the Tampa boatpeople with the rape epidemic. Betts, "Immigration and public opinion: understanding the shift," pp 33-34.

[361] Claire Adida, David. Laitin, and Marie Anne Valfori, *Why Muslim Integration Fails in Christian Heritage Societies* (Cambridge MA: Harvard University Press, 2016).

[362] Paul M. Sniderman and Louk. Hagendoorn, *When Ways of Life Collide: Multiculturalism and Its Discontents in the Netherlands* (Princeton, NJ: Princeton University Press, 2007).

[363] Charles Miller, "Australia's anti-Islam right in their own words. A text as data analysis of social media content," *Australian Journal of Political Science* 52, no. 383-401 (2017): p 386.

[364] Joint Standing Committee on Migration, "Inquiry into Migration and Multiculturalism in Australia," (The Parliament of the Commonwealth of Australia, 2013), p 64. Footnote 47.

[365] This was at the Cumberland Council run Ruth Everuss Aquatic Centre where a retractable curtain was installed around one of three pools so Muslim women could swim privately during two time slots on Wednesdays.

the face except for the eyes".[366] Other specific instances have included the principal and deputy at the largely Muslim Punchbowl Boys High School who were reported as being "dumped" amid a backlash over the exclusion of female teachers at official school events.[367] The head of the NSW Department of Education, Mark Scott, said this school seems to have "lost its way in recent times and become more isolated from the community."[368] The Hurstville Boys High introduced a protocol whereby male Muslim students were allowed to decline shaking hands with women in accordance with an "ancient Islamic hadith".[369] The Education Minister, Rob Stokes, called the protocol "sexist".[370] At the University of Western Sydney's Parramatta campus, the MSA requested the segregation of men and women at an event. The Vice-Chancellor, Professor Barney Glover, was quoted as saying that the MSA's request was a "mistake".[371]

Women's interests under Sharia law have lately come under public scrutiny. The ABC's recent feature *'I'm not his property': Abused Muslim women denied right to divorce* referred to "experts" who say that the "'crux' of the issue … is the fact that the laws governing Islamic divorce in Australia are based on deeply conservative, patriarchal interpretations of Islam, which means women's rights are ultimately ignored".[372]

---

[366] Khan Anisa, interview by Monique. Schaffer and Jeanavive McGregor21 October 2014. The wearing of full facial veils has been banned in public across Western Europe, including in France and the Netherlands.

[367] Rebecca Urban, "Troubled Punchbowl Boys High School leadership team dumped," *The Australian*, 3 March 2017. Urban wrote that tensions at the school had been building since the new principal Mr Griffiths took over from Mr Jihad Dib in late 2015.

[368] "Punchbowl School 'resisted ' Islam program," *The Australian*, 6 March 2017.

[369] Samuel Osborne, "Australian school allows male Muslim pupils to refuse handshakes with women," *Independent*, 20 February 2017.

[370] Urban, "Troubled Punchbowl Boys High School leadership team dumped.")

[371] Barney Glover, "Challenging cultural and social divides," *The Daily Telegraph*, 21 May 2015.

[372] Hayley Gleeson and Julia Baird, "'I'm not his property': Abused Muslim women denied right to divorce," (2018).

Specifically, in Australia:

> Islamic law (sharia) operates in the shadow of the official legal system
> and the all-male imams who administer it with impunity. Muslim
> women's right to leave a marriage is not always recognised.[373] ...
> Compounding the problem, social workers and survivors say, is the
> fact that many imams are ignorant or dismissive of the dynamics
> and seriousness of domestic violence.[374]

Not only Muslim clerics are "dismissive", so are some community leaders. AFIC President, Keysar Trad, told Andrew Bolt on Sky News in February 2017 that "beating a women was 'step three' in a process of dealing with a relationship", and Studio 10 "it was a last resort".[375] Sheik Nawas was reported on the ABC feature as saying that the reason for the high rate of applications by women for divorce to the Board of Imams in Victoria is domestic violence.[376]

More generally, the ABC feature stated that a "consistent theme in public pronouncements by imams ... is that men have the authority to control the movements and actions of their wives, and that women must obey and respect their husbands without qualification."[377]

---

[373] The ABC quoted Dr Anisa Buckley as saying "[t]he biggest obstacle ... facing Muslim women in securing religious divorce is the belief across communities, families and religious leaders ... that Muslim women require their husband's consent when seeking to initiate divorce, and have limited grounds upon which to initiate divorce". Ibid., p 17. Another "significant barrier is the view of many Muslims that women should strive to keep the family together no matter how difficult or dangerous the situation". Ibid., p19

[374] Ibid., p 4. "The shame and stigma surrounding domestic violence can prevent many women from leaving". Ibid., p 22. Moreover, "while many Muslim leaders and imams in Australia are consistent in their denouncing of physical violence, what is less clear is their approach to emotional, psychological, financial and sexual abuse". Ibid., p 11.

[375] Trad later "'apologised" for condoning domestic violence, calling his interpretation of the Quran 'clumsy'". Omar Darbagh, SBS News, 24 Febtuary, 2017. He also appeared on other networks to denounce domestic violence "unequivocally".

[376] Gleeson and Baird, "'I'm not his property': Abused Muslim women denied right to divorce". p 4. 95 per cent of such applications are made by women.

[377] Ibid., p 22.

The acclaimed author Larry Siedentorp argues that "Muslims are frequently encouraged to look forward to replacing the laws of the nation-state with sharia 'law'".[378] In 2011, AFIC President Ikebal Patel called on "Australia to compromise with Islam and embrace legal pluralism".[379]

The University of New South Wales' and Macquarie University's *Racism Survey*, that was reported on by Kevin Dunn, Natascha Klocker and Tanya Salabay, found that "women were much more likely to communicate concern" if one of their "relative[s] were to marry a Muslim than a Jew, Christian or persons from an ... Asian background".[380]

A social value shared by Western secular societies, such the Netherlands, France and Australia, is freedom of speech. But following the deadly *Charlie Hebdo* attack in Paris; addressing 800-1,000 placard waving protestors in front of the Lakemba war memorial, Sufyan Badar, a spokesman for Hizb ut-Tahrir, told the crowd: "Muslims should not accept or embrace the freedom of speech preached by the West and urged those present to reject it".[381]

While the above surveys, media reports, ABC features, public comments and the like receive extensive coverage on prime time

---

[378] Larry Siedentorp, *Inventing the Individual The Origins of Western Liberalism* (Penguin, 2014), p 350.

[379] Chris Merritt, "Sharia law at work in Australia," *The Australian*, 20 July 2011. Patel was reported as facing a "backlash [from] inside the Muslim community".

[380] Kevin M Dunn, Natascha Klocker, and Tanya Salabay, "Contemporary racism and Islamophobia in Australia: Racializing religion," *Ethnicities* 7, no. 4 (2007): p 573. Dunn et al. were disappointed that the "level of concern regarding Muslims was well above other 'out groups'".

[381] Andrew Carswell and Ian Walker, "Sydney's Muslim community rallies in Lakemba in response to terror attacks that rocked Paris," *The Daily Telegraph*, 23 January 2015.

television, radio news, current affairs programs and talk back radio,[382] they are more confronting for long standing locals living in western Sydney where they mostly occurred than in the inner-city electorate of Sydney with a barely noticeable 2.1 per cent Muslim population and Grayndler with less at 1.6 per cent.[383] Thus Sheik Tajuddin Hilaly, *Mufti* of Australia's Muslims, in a 2006 sermon delivered in front of around 500 worshipers at the Lakemba mosque said women who do not wear a hijab (which usually covers the head and chest) were like "uncovered meat" left out for cats.[384] The BBC's Nick Bryant noted that the "clerics latest comments[385] are seen as particularly insensitive because [western] Sydney was the scene six years ago of a series of gang rapes committed by a group of Lebanese Australians",[386] which caused anxiety and fear among many local non-Muslim girls and women. The Crown Prosecutor at the trials, Margaret Cunneen, said that these "crimes had left an indelible stain on the psyche of the citizens of NSW".[387] Yet the research project *Islamophobia in Australia* (which was conducted to provide evidence and arguments in support of their report's claim of institutional and individual racism towards

---

[382] Tom Switzer, "Why Muslims make headlines," in *Islam and the Australian News Media*, ed. Halim. Rane, Jacqui. Ewart, and Mohamad. Abdalla (2010), p 124.

[383] Percentages calculated from data in ABS (2016) *Commonwealth Electoral Divisions*.

[384] Mark Tran, "Australian Muslim leader compares uncovered women to exposed meat " *The Guardian* 26 October 2006. On the Thursday following the report in *The Australian* on 25 October 2006, Hilaly released a statement which read: "I unreservedly apologize to any woman who is offended by my comments. I had only intended to protect women's honour, something lost in *The Australian* presentation of my talk." Keysar Trad, a spokesman for Sheik Hilaly, had earlier said that "[t]he issue is about extra-marital sexual activity. [Sheik Hilaly] was not talking about rape." Keysar Trad, interview by Josie Talor26 October 2006. Janet Albrechtsen reported that "when the sheik returned to Lakemba mosque … 5000 people turned up to listen and cheer." Janet. Albrechtsen, *The Australian* 1 November 2006.

[385] Sheik Hilaly was known for his public outbursts of racial intolerance – particularly towards Jews.

[386] "Australia fury at cleric comments", BBC News Online, 26 October 2006.

[387] "Rapist out of sight but not out of mind", The Age Online, August 2, 2003.

Muslims in Australia) was bewildered by its own finding that, "of the 120 incidents where information about the location of the incident [of Islamophobia] was available, 48.3% ... occurred in multicultural diverse [suburbs]" – as are the suburbs of western Sydney – saying "people [there] are presumably more exposed to different ethno-religious backgrounds".[388]

The Committee on Migration noted that cultural tensions and Shari'ah courts in Europe were "widely cited as the direct consequence of the proportional increase in Islamic populations in these regions".[389] In an address to The Sydney Institute, the Minister for Immigration and Citizenship in the Gillard Government, Chris Bowen, said only 1.71 per cent of the Australian population identify ... themselves as Muslims".[390] But by 2050 Muslims are projected to grow to "5 per cent of the Australian population,[391] making Islam the second largest religion".[392]

The actual experience with migration and cultural diversity policies of long standing locals in Sydney's outer western suburbs were obviously ignored by both the elites and governments.

Barry Cohen, a Minister in the Whitlam Government, wrote that the initial government policy of "assimilation got the heave-ho because

---

[388] Derya (ed.) Iner, "Islamophobia in Australia," (Charles Sturt University, 2017), p 53.

[389] Joint Standing Committee on Migration, "Inquiry into Migration and Multiculturalism in Australia," p 70.

[390] Chris Bowen, "The genius of Australian multiculturalism," *The Sydney Institute* (2011).

[391] This was the percentage of the Muslim population in England in 2015. Aisha Gani, *The Guardian*, 12 February 2015.

[392] The Preliminary Islamophobia Report forecasts that the "population of Australian Muslims ... will grow fourfold over the next four decades. Riaz Hassan and Bill Martin, "Islamophobia, social distance and fear of terrorism in Australia: A Preliminary Report," (University of South Australia, 2015), p 43.

the *ethnic lobby* thought it insulting [italics added].[393] Immigrants, they said, should remain exactly as they were when they arrived and the government should fund them to do so."[394] Mark Lopez, author of the only comprehensive history of Australian multiculturalism, supported Cohen's claim of an "ethnic lobby", arguing that multiculturalism was developed by a small number of Anglo-Australian academics, social workers and activists initially on the fringe of the political arena; "the overwhelming majority of ethnic groups and their leaders played no direct role in the progress of multiculturalism".[395] Jerzy Zubrycki, an "intellectual architect" of multiculturalism during the early 1970s, later reflected: "[m]ulticulturalism is a good idea that has gone wrong. Ethnicity has been cynically exploited for electoral ... advantage" and "social engineering".[396]

In her 1999 book, *The Great Divide: Immigration Policies in Australia*, Katherine Betts revealed:

> In 1977 more than two fifths of the electorate thought that current levels of immigration were too high and by the mid-1980s the proportion had risen to two thirds. Despite this adverse public opinion and despite the lack of tangible benefits for the Australian people, the immigration figures grew from 1976 to 1988 until the net intake was higher than at any other time in the post-war

---

[393] Professor Andrew Markus and Margaret Taft argue that "[t]here was no significant development in assimilation policy over the course of the 1950s. Yet had there been substantial planning and resource allocation, the policy would still have been destined for failure. As ... short-term assimilation under government regimentation is 'impossible of achievement for larger groups of people'." Andrew Markus and Margaret Taft, "Postwar Immigration and Assimilation: A Reconceptualisation," *Australian Historical Studies* 46, no. 2 (2015): p 250-1.

[394] Barry Cohen, *The Australian*, 24 October 1996.

[395] Mark Lopez, "The Politics of the Origins of Multiculturalism," *People and Place* 8, no. 1 (2000): p 23.

[396] Jerzy Zubrycki, *The Australian*, 15 October 1996.

period.[397]

In part Betts attributed federal governments' indifference to any potential for a voter backlash to a "tacit bipartisan pact between the two major political parties not to make immigration an election issue. ... This allowed *political elites* to ignore public opinion and press ahead with large intakes despite their unpopularity [italics added]."[398]

Healy and Birrell note that the "metropolitan cultural elites" have embraced ethnic concentrations, insisting this "diversity now represents what is 'truly' Australian".[399]

The "political and economic elites" are, as Betts and Birrell argue, disdainful of the discontent among ordinary voters with Australia's immigration policy, and so they just ignore them. "They see high immigration as part of their commitment to the globalisation of Australia's economy and society and thus it is not to be questioned. ... Elites elsewhere in the developed world hold similar views, but have had to retreat because of public opposition. Across Europe 15 to 20 per cent of voters currently support anti-immigration political parties."[400]

The foregoing analysis suggests that Labor should urgently reconsider the ideology and agenda of multiculturalism, while at the same time reaffirming Labor's commitment to the multicultural society that ordinary Australians accepted. It should be seen to play an important part in the public debate as to the level of migrant intake.

[397] Katharine Betts, *The Great Divide: Immigration Politics in Australia* (Sydney, NSW: Duffy and Snellgrove, 1999), p 3.

[398] Bob Hawke "thought that the theory about how the major parties had developed an implicit pact not to treat immigration as an electoral issue and had quietly colluded in high immigration without consulting the electorate was a 'brilliant insight'". Ibid., p 6.

[399] Healy and Birrell, "Metropolis divided: The political dynamics of spatial inequality and migrant settlement in Sydney," p 83.

[400] Betts and Birrell, "Australian voters' views' on immigration policy," p v.

It should continue with the services government provides to new arrivals – particularly English language courses so they can successfully integrate into Australian society – especially to those fleeing civil war zones. The importance of English language to successful integration is well established. As Ian Burnley and his co-authors point out:

> A connection between strong ethnic residential concentration, high unemployment and therefore disadvantage is the degree of English language proficiency. Higher proportions of people not speaking English well were evident in the Lebanese ... core concentrations in Sydney, notably among women, and higher levels of unemployment were experienced in these concentrations as well, more especially with women. Persons with less spoken English or capacity to read it have less chance of obtaining information about opportunities in their wider environment, or of obtaining work.[401]

But while recognising that "Muslims have been 'challenged deeply' by European modernity, facing a mammoth task in relating Islam to modern life",[402] Labor should also consider the effects on "social cohesion" from a clash of "social values" that is evident in the findings of public opinion surveys, and in western Sydney's experience with "cultural or social etiquettes", with women's place and interests under Sharia law, and with the at times egregious public utterances of senior Muslim clerics and community leaders – which are only recanted after being "called out" by the mainstream media.[403] In doing so, Labor should be alert to the divisive influence on public debate of the "socially

---

[401] Ian Burnley, Peter Murphy, and Robert Fagan, *Immigration and Australian Capital Cities* (Leichhardt, NSW: Federation Press, 1997), p 56.

[402] Mehmet Ozalp, Director of the Centre for Islamic Studies and Civilisation at Charles Sturt University, Joint Standing Committee on Migration, "Inquiry into Migration and Multiculturalism in Australia," p 68.

[403] Similarly, several high profile members of the Muslim community were critical of Sheik Hilaly's remarks, with the Islamic Council of Victoria's Waleed Aly reported as calling the content of the sermon repugnant. But these community leaders only came out after *The Australian* published Hilaly's sermon.

progressive new class" referred to by Betts as having developed politically correct attitudes towards immigration to symbolise their distance from ordinary Australians.[404] They comprise the "New Left counter-culture" movements who Lopez noted "identified racism as a central feature of the 'Australian character'".[405]

Then there is Robert Manne, who in an article for *The Age* titled "Beware the new racism",[406] accused Australia of being far from "immune" to the ideological "virus" of Islamophobia.[407] "Islamophobia now represents the most serious threat to the idea of multiculturalism".[408] However, for Nick Haslam the notion of Islamophobia "brushes aside opinions we dislike by invalidating the people who hold them ... clos[ing] the door[409]on dialogue" and on debate.[410]

[404] Betts, *The Great Divide: Immigration Politics in Australia*, p 10.

[405] Mark Lopez, *The Origins of Multiculturalism in Australian Politics 1945-1975* (Carlton South, Vic.: Melbourne University Press, 2000), p 83.

[406] Robert Manne, "Beware the new racism," *The Age*, 16 September 2002. Manne claimed that sociologists have uncovered a "new racism", "Islamophobia". They argue the "difference between human collectives [are] based on the ultimate incompatibility not of blood and biology but of culture and religion".

[407] Manne's choice of the words "immune" and "virus" is deplorable, as they echo metaphors used in Germany during the 1930s.

[408] Robert Manne, "Open Season on Muslims in the Newest Phobia," *Sydney Morning Herald*, 16 September 2002.

[409] Nick Haslam, "Bigots are just sick at heart," *The Australian*, 17 December 2008. An example of this "closing the door" is the case of Ayaan Hirsi Ali – a former Muslim considered to be an "apostate" in her country of birth, Somali, who cancelled her proposed April 2017 speaking tour of Australia in the face of the Council for the Prevention of Islamophobia informing the organisers that there would be 5,000 protestors outside Melbourne's Festival Hall if Hirsi Ali were to speak at the venue. Paul. Maly, "Islam critic Ayaan Hirsi Ali cancels tour," ibid. 4 April 2017.

[410] Brian McNair wrote that "critiquing Islam [is not] Islamophobia [nor] racism [nor is it] anti-Muslim". Brian McNair, "Islam and the media - let's not fear open debate," (2015), The Conversation, online.

Labor's "forgotten people"

Crisp, as Director-General of Post-War Reconstruction, was one of Prime Minister Chifley's closest advisers. Writing a few years after the 1979 Inquiry, he and many of his ALP friends in various states were profoundly concerned by the consequences of a "widespread takeover or substantial takeover of local branches" by professionals and white-collar employees. Based on his experience, Crisp attributed the "takeover" to:

> both Anglo-Saxon and ethnic Australian blue-collar feeling - and, let us confess, usually justifiable feeling - discouraged from participating in ALP branch life and discussions. Many of their white-collar members do show (however thoughtlessly) impatience with some blue-collar agenda items or are dismissive of the blue-collar contributions to debates on other items.[411]

The "takeover" led to:

> a substantial withdrawal of the blue collars from all sorts of branches ... Over and over again I hear of the spread of this blue-collar withdrawal. Some blue-collars withdraw right into the privacy of the family circle and the company of blue-collar neighbourhoods ... Others withdraw at least into the union branches, or into the local licensed clubs.[412]

Andrew Scott argues that the erosion of working class support has caused Labor to become so "unrepresentative of Labor voters that they become unlikely to preselect anyone for parliament who lacks the polished communication skills of the professionally trained".[413] Dyrenfurth traced Labor's poor record in preselecting working class candidates to the "late 1960s 'Whitlamite' Party revolution", which he

---

[411] Crisp, "The Labor Party: Then and Now," p 77.
[412] Ibid., pp 72-3.
[413] Scott, *Fading loyalties: The Australian Labor Party and the Working Class*, p 57.

argues "has gone too far".[414]

Bowen's response to Scott's and Dyrenfurth's concerns with Labor's failure to preselect working class candidates is to say:

> Ben Chifley today would almost certainly not have become an engine driver. Ben Chifley did not go to university because it was unheard of in his day for a child of the working class to darken the door of a university. Now thanks to Whitlam's abolition of university fees, thanks to Hawke and Keating's introduction of the Higher Education Contribution Scheme and thanks to Rudd and Gillard's massive expansion of university places, young Ben Chifley may well become a lawyer, doctor, engineer or economist.[415]

However, a recent study titled *Youth Unemployment in Western Sydney* casts serious doubt on Bowen's contention, as it found that "Western Sydney youth have lower rates of school completion and bachelor degree attainment ... than elsewhere in Sydney".[416] Similarly, another recent study titled *What Price the Gap? Education and Inequality in Australia* found that "[e]ducation inequality is increasing across a wide range of dimensions" in Australia. But that "socio-economic status and parental education are the main drivers for educational inequality, while Australia performs relatively well on gender and migrant status which are problematic in other countries". Moreover, the study states that "it is widely understood that Australia's school performance ... has been falling. What's less understood is that ... kids at the bottom of the performance distribution are falling faster and further than

[414] Dyrenfurth, "It's time Labor went back to the workers."
[415] Bowen, *Hearts & Minds: A Blueprint for Modern Labor*, p 11.
[416] P O'Neill, "Youth Unemployment in Western Sydney," (Centre for Western Sydney, 2017), p 8.

kids at the top".[417]

Cavalier's view on the Party's failure to preselect working class candidates is altogether different than Bowen's. According to his interpretation of Karl Marx, there is no working class! "The working class is a stratum of society oppressed by the means of production, distribution and exchange, the stratum is conscious of that oppression and acts in concert with others in the stratum similarly oppressed in order to end the oppression".[418] Although Cavalier allows that "[t]he poor and the disadvantaged have not ceased to exist. Nor have a majority of this stratum ceased to vote for Labor." [419] In other words, Cavalier attributes the paucity of working class candidates to their lack of class consciousness. But for Marx, a person's class is determined entirely by their relationship to the means of production (i.e. their relations of production). And Marx's definition does not exclude those who cannot work.

The term working class is defined and used differently by social scientists, journalists, historians and more commonly. But a contemporary Australian working class would include blue collar industrial workers (mostly men), routine white collar workers in the services sector (mostly women, many of who work part-time), the long term unemployed (i.e. those who only have their labour to sell) – and, I would add, homemakers from low socio-economic backgrounds – which constitutes approximately 58 per cent of the

---

[417] David Hetherington, "What Price the Gap? Education and Inequality in Australia," (Public Education Foundation, 2018), p 3. The study estimated that "over the six years from 2009-15 alone, this growing inequality has cost Australia around $20.3 billion, equivalent to 1.2% of GDP. The longer-term cost to Australia is even bigger, because the gap was widening well prior to 2009."

[418] Rodney Cavalier, "There is no working class," *Southern Highlands Branch Newsletter* 1999.

[419] Ibid.

civilian population aged 15 years and over.[420]

However, Cavalier is on to something in so far as this contemporary working class does not have a public voice with which to air their aspirations and grievances, other than on talk-back radio. They do not appear on television (other than when portrayed as carriers of social pathologies, as in the initial episode of the SBS's *Struggle Street*), nor in the opinion pages of the major metropolitan newspapers. Moreover, as Christopher Scanlon writes, Labor politicians:

> only rarely use the term [class] and, when they do, it is used more as a rhetorical device than a means to say anything substantive about the nature of contemporary social and economic life.
>
> In policy papers, press conferences and doorstop interviews, Labor politicians prefer phrases such as "working families" and "working people" rather than "working class". The beauty of working people and working families is that they gesture towards social and economic distinctions, but in a way that glosses over uncomfortable questions about how those divisions are produced and maintained.[421]

Bramble and Kuhn would in part at least put their reticence down to the "election of Whitlam [that] marked the advent of a new generation of Labor leaders ... Of subsequent Labor leaders only Bill Hayden ... had sustained experience in anything approximating a working class job", and that the "changes in the background of

---

[420] Percentages calculated from data in ABS *Labour Force Australia* 6202.0 as at May 2017. Using ABS Labour Force Australia 6202.0 as at May 2017, this figure was arrived at by subtracting the Managerial (1,543.9) and Professional (2,858.7) classifications from the Employed total persons (12,205.9) to give a figure for the employed working class of 7,805.3. To this figure was added Females not in the labour force (4,060.5) deflated by 25 per cent, to give a figure for working class homemakers of 3,045.4, and the Unemployed total persons (703.4) to give a total of 11552.1 for the employed working class + working class homemakers + the long term unemployed. The civilian population aged 15 and over (19,829.2) was then divided by this total to give an approximate percentage of 58 for the contemporary Australian working class.

[421] Christopher Scanlon, "A touch of class," *The Age*, 17 April 2004.

leaders were mirrored in the parliamentary caucus." [422] They also commented on the personal benefits politicians enjoy, in the form of high salaries, perks and pensions, which sets them apart from workers.[423] Thus the "current life experience of Labor MPs is hardly likely to give them insights into workers' lives'".[424]

Moreover, as Thomas Piketty argues, the party system in the 1950s-1960s was "class based". But that, "[s]ince the 1970s-1980s, the 'left-wing' vote has gradually become associated with higher education voters ... high-education elites now vote for the 'left', while the high income/high wealth elites still vote for the 'right' (although less and less so). ... [T]he "left" has become the Party of the intellectual elite ... [T]he same transformation happened in France, the US and Britain ... despite the many differences in Party systems and political histories between these three countries."[425]

This "transformation" happened in Australia, too. Beginning in the mid-1970s, this antipodean "elite" pointed to the declining numbers of industrial workers and claimed that supporters of feminism, multiculturalism, environmentalism and the like superseded the working class as Labor's base vote. The Party has subsequently informally recognised Rainbow Labor, LEAN and other interest groups. Their influence on Labor's policies was on show at recent Party national conferences. In an address to the 2011 National Conference on marriage equality, Faulkner thundered: "[h]uman rights can never be at the mercy of individual opinions or individual

---

[422] Bramble and Kuhn, "Continuity or Discontinuity in the Recent History of the Australian Labor Party?," p 284.

[423] Ibid.

[424] Ibid., p 286.

[425] Thomas Piketty, "Brahmin Left v Merchant Right: Rising Inequality & the Changing Structure of Political Conflict," (World Inequality Database, 2018), p 3.

prejudices".[426] The *Sydney Morning Herald* listed climate change, gay marriage and asylum seekers among the "six big issues to be debated at Labor's [2015] national conference".[427] Little was said about the unemployment in Sydney's outer western and like suburbs in other states and territories, with the notable exception of Unions NSW Secretary, Mark Lennon. The 2018 *ALP National Platform Consultation Draft*[428] that was to be debated at the 2018 National Conference mentioned "bisexual" 31 times, LGBTI 21 times, LGBTIQ 15 times, "intersex" (intersex being the "I" in LGBTI and LGBTIQ) 61 times, "intersexphobia" and intersexphobic" once each in the 211 page draft document. "Refugee" was mentioned 39 times, and "climate change" 80 times.[429]

Faulkner's call for activists never to be outside the Labor movement is consistent with the academic suggestion of a more "diverse" notion of "modern membership" that reaches out beyond joining a local branch to embrace "advocacy groups". The success of Labor parliamentarians supportive of groups such as LEAN and Rainbow Labor is evidenced by their influence at national conferences during the last decade and a half. Paul Kelly reported from the 2018 National Conference that LEAN "was prominent at the previous conference in securing a 50 per cent renewable energy target. It was influential at this conference in securing the rewriting of environmental law and the creation of a proposed federal

[426] Marriage Equality – 46th ALP National Conference 2011 Senator John Faulkner Sydney Convention and Exhibition Centre, Darling Harbour, December 2011.

[427] Matthew. Knott and Adam. Gartrell, "The six big issues to be debated at Labor's national conference," *Sydney Morning Herald* 24 July 2015.)

[428] ALP, "ALP National Platform Consultation Draft," (April 2018).

[429] Adam Creighton undertook a more extensive exercise to highlight the influence of identity politics on Labor. Adam Creighton, "Labor's identity politics - the left's blight on the hill," *The Australian*, 30 April 2018. The 2018 Platform does talk up apprenticeship, and the commissioning of yet another review of higher education.

environmental protection authority".[430] 15 years ago frontbencher, and former ALP National President, Jenny McAllister, formed LEAN "in a pioneering move that introduces activist lobbies into the party".[431] McAllister told Kelly it is "'incredible' to see the growth in LEAN members at conference and to know there is a group coming from ALP branches around the country".[432]

The Howard Government's *Marriage Amendment Act 2004* defined marriage as a "union of a man and a woman to the exclusion of all others"; it was supported by both major political parties, with no public dissent. During the 2010 election campaign, Prime Minister Julia Gillard stated that her government would not sponsor or support any bill to legislate for same-sex marriage. However, at the Party's 2011 National Conference, Labor endorsed an amendment to the Party's Platform in support of legalising same-sex marriage. A motion, sponsored by Prime Minister Gillard, was also passed allowing MPs and Senators a free vote on same-sex marriage legislation. At the 2015 National Conference, the motion to continue the free vote on same-sex marriage legislation was lost, however a period of grace was granted for the existing and next parliamentary terms, but after the 2019 federal election MPs and Senators would be bound by Party policy to support same-sex marriage legislation. Anthony Albanese, Penny Wong and Tanya Plibersek were instrumental behind the scenes in changing the Platform in 2011, but the activities of Rainbow Labor were also influential. The Party's national conferences provide the opportunity for powerful parliamentary figures within the Party to shape Labor's policies in keeping with interest group thinking.

---

[430] Paul Kelly, "Bill's fixes fine for opposition, but not government," ibid. 19 December 2018. Although, "it failed to secure a more ambitious agenda from the environmental spokesman, Tony Burke".

[431] Ibid.

[432] Ibid.

Not for the Party's national conferences the NSW Parliamentary Research Service's 2014 table of electoral districts ranked by their unemployment rate that shows, of the ten with the highest unemployment levels, six were in Sydney's western suburbs: Fairfield, Cabramatta, Lakemba, Bankstown, Liverpool and Auburn, while lying just outside the ten at number 13 was Mount Druitt.[433] The *Youth Unemployment in Western Sydney's* report showed that "youth unemployment is significantly higher in Sydney's west than elsewhere in Greater Sydney".[434] It identified 23 geographic clusters of youth unemployment within Western Sydney "where the rate of youth unemployment (15 to 24 years) ranges from 16.4% to an upper extreme of 26.4% and where the rate of young unemployment (15 to 19 years) ranges from 23% to a top of 36.5%". It found that "the average levels of disengagement in employment and education in Western Sydney exceed those in non-Western Sydney".[435] The Commonwealth Parliamentary Library's *Index of Relative Socio-economic Disadvantage*[436] for the 2009 electoral divisions which show that the "ten divisions with the "high[est] proportion of relative disadvantaged people in an area"[437] include four in NSW: Fowler (which includes the suburbs of Liverpool and Cabramatta), Blaxland (which includes the suburbs of Bankstown and Auburn), Chifley (which includes the suburbs of Mount Druitt and Rooty Hill) and Watson (which includes the suburb of Lakemba and parts of Canterbury).[438]

Nor for the 2010 Review targeting voters lost or attracted to

---

[433] Daniel Montoya and Jack Finegan, "Background Paper No 04/2014," (NSW Parliamentary Research Service, 2014), p 107.

[434] "[A]side from the Central coast" – which is also a working class demographic.

[435] O'Neill, "Youth Unemployment in Western Sydney," pp 7-8.

[436] Paul Nelson, "Socio-economic indexes for 2009 electoral divisions: 2006 Census," (Parliamentary Library, 2010), p 3.

[437] The index refers to the "lowest ranking", and "a low score on the index indicates a high proportion of relative disadvantaged people in an area". Ibid.

[438] Ibid., p 6.

"right wing populist parties with a largely anti-immigrant agenda". Its recommendations focused soley on targeting voters lost or attracted to the Greens. The 2010 Review commented that the Greens' primary vote increased to a record 11.8 per cent at the 2010 election. But the Greens' vote stalled badly at the two subsequent federal elections. Their 2016 result for the Senate showed a fall of 0.58 per cent (with its primary vote at 8.65 per cent), while Pauline Hanson's One Nation Party's vote was up 3.76 per cent,[439] which saw it for the first time win seats outside of its base in rural and regional Queensland, one each in NSW and WA for a total of four Senators. Further, as reported in *The Guardian*, a Newspoll survey taken between 6 and 9 October 2016 showed that "One Nation would win 6% of the national vote in the House of Representatives (which compares with 1.3 per cent at the 2 July election)". According to the survey, "One Nation has reached 10% lower house support in Queensland (up from 5.5% at the election), and it would win 6% of the vote in the lower house in NSW and WA."[440] Another Newspoll reported in *The Australian* on 27 February 2017 showed that "[d]isaffected voters have driven Pauline Hanson's One Nation to 10 per cent of the primary vote, more than doubling that Party's support since November" – putting its electoral support equal to that of the Greens.[441] Then there is the Greens failure to take the federal seat of Batman as expected at the 2018 by-election. While more recently, the Green's performed disastrously at the 2018 Victorian state election.

The foregoing analysis suggests that Labor should turn a deaf ear to intellectual elites and cease fretting over Green sympathisers;

---

[439] http://results.aec.gov.au/20499/Website/SenateStateFirstPrefsByGroup-20499-NAT.htm

[440] Paul Karp, "Pauline Hanson's One Nation triples support since election: Newspoll," *The Guardian*, 17 October 2016.

[441] David Crowe, "Newspoll: Coalition on slide as voters turn to Pauline Hanson," *The Australian*, 27 February 2017.

instead, a top policy priority for Labor should be tackling the youth unemployment that is endemic to socio-economically disadvantaged suburbs of western Sydney and like suburbs in other states and territories. As the Party's Platform has no clear statement on unemployment, a symbolic start for Labor should be to adopt wording similar to the duty of the Reserve Bank's Board, which includes ensuring its powers are exercised in such a manner as will best contribute to the maintenance of full employment.[442] Labor should also make equality in school and higher education for the low SES another top policy priority. To these ends, the Party should target for preselection to safe Labor seats working class members – especially women – who represent the opinions and experience of voters in their electorates.

---

[442] *Reserve Bank Act 1959* (Cth), section 10(2) of which is often referred to as the Bank's "charter". The charter provides that: It is the duty of the Reserve Bank Board, within the limits of its powers, to ensure that the monetary and banking policy of the Bank is directed to the greatest advantage of the people of Australia and that the powers of the Bank are exercised in such a manner as, in the opinion of the Reserve Bank Board, will best contribute to: a. the stability of the currency of Australia; b. the maintenance of full employment in Australia; and c. the economic prosperity and welfare of the people of Australia.

CONCLUSION

The Reviews' recommendations for structural reform were relatively "minor". The major change made by the Party has been affirmative action for women, with Labor committed to equal parliamentary representation for women by 2025. AYL now has 3 of the 400 delegates to national conference. Ethnic communities must be satisfied with branch stacking, and some cases of intervention. Members directly elect 150 delegates to national conference. The 60-40 rule for union delegates' representation at state conferences has been reduced to 50-50.

Right and left union leaders will continue to oppose any proposals by Faulkner and others to further reduce their representation at state conferences, which effectively means that for the time being the unions will retain their dominance within the Party, while the right will oppose any such moves so as to effectively stop the left's attempts at gaining control of the Party.

By their own admissions, Ray's and Dyrenfurth's proposals for the factions to drive Party renewal lack a certain flavour of reality. Still, if Ray's Caucus brimming full with talent – such as the one that coalesced under Bill Hayden's parliamentary leadership – were to materialise any time soon, the ideological "glue" to hold it together could be opposition to the "regressive left". The degeneration of the factions has also led to the rise of a political class that today pervades Labor's preselections for safe seats, who are only interest in power, and whose hold on power will only be loosened by the Party adopting Cavalier's or Dyrenfurth's proposals to restrict their ilk from standing for preselection ballots. However, unless the popular disaffection with the political class that is beginning to be seen in Australia was to dramatically increase, as in the UK and US, the Party will not entertain any such proposal (or any policy that targets working class candidates for preselection to safe Labor seats). Baldwin warns of the left-wing, progressive's embrace of identity politics, which sees threats to freedom of speech by allegations of racism and the like, as well, it is behind the failure of federal governments to address the serious economic problems confronting Australia today, and the sidelining of working class aspirations and grievances as the focus of Labor policy.

Scholarly analyses suggests that, notwithstanding the Party's days as a mass party are behind it, Labor can survive as a major political force into the foreseeable future by means of taxpayer funding, private donations, modern professional campaigning and personalised leadership – along with the following default electoral tactics: the electoral cycle ("It's time"), making itself a small target (as Kim Beazley tried in 1998 and 2001), adopting scare campaigns (as Bill Shorten tried in 2016), and forming a minority government (as Julia Gillard did in 2010). But adopting those tactics will mean Labor governments being unable to carry the Australian electorate on any policy it proposes in the face of stiff opposition.

The 2010 Review pivoted from the 2002 Review's concern with regaining the loyalty of Labor's traditional working class supporters to focus on voters lost or attracted to the Greens. But contrary to what the 2010 Review suggests, the real threat to Labor comes not from the Greens, most of whose voters live in a few inner capital city electorates (and as inner city property prices periodically soar, most of these inner city seats could fall to Liberal Party candidates). Nor does it come from One Nation, if for no other reason than that to date it has never mounted a national election campaign. However, consistent with concerns raised by the 2002 Review, the on going threat comes from a Liberal federal parliamentary leader like John Howard who can – over the head of the mainstream media – appeal directly to "social conservative" Australians, including to "large swaths of traditional Labor voters".

But there is no Liberal parliamentarian on the horizon with Howard's ability or instincts. So notwithstanding Bill Shorten's standing in the polls, Labor is favoured to win the upcoming federal election. Irrespective, the influence of identity politics on Labor's policy formation is the "existential" threat facing Labor today. Activists who prosecute the agendas associated with its theories by means of their privileged access to the Party's conferences, Platform and powerful Labor parliamentarians – and who are aided and abetted by the political class' ideological agnosticism. If it fails to come to terms with identity politics, sooner or later the Party risks inflicting a permanent electoral setback on Labor by fostering an anti-politician who can appeal to the urban working class as successfully as has Pauline Hanson to rural and regional Australia – to women from low socio-economic backgrounds who benefited little from the Reviews; to older asset poor Australians who Labor has turned its back on; to longstanding locals in socio-economically disadvantaged suburbs living with issues of Muslim integration and acute ethnic concentrations that show every sign of being an enduring feature of Sydney's west; and to working class youths in western Sydney facing dire employment and educational prospects. If that anti-politician's policy priority is, as Ben Chifley's was, in seeing that "all the community are in a position to have a decent standard of living",[443] and they tackle the difficult and complex economic circumstances that Australia finds itself in today, as Hawke and Keating did in their day, rather than being those of protest that do not work when in government, then it may be that the ALP's days as a political party that can win office in its own right will have come to an end.

---

[443] Ben Chifley, "These things are really worth fighting for," in *Annual Conference of the NSW Branch* (1948).

BIBLIOGRAPHY

ACTU. "Labor Party review reaffirms unions as the "bedrock" of the modern ALP." news release, 18 February, 2011.

Adida, Claire, David. Laitin, and Marie Anne Valfori. *Why Muslim Integration Fails in Christian Heritage Societies*. Cambridge MA: Harvard University Press, 2016.

Albrechtsen, Janet. *The Australian*, 1 November 2006.

Allan, Lyle. "Ethnic Recruitment or Ethnic Branch Stacking?: Factionalism and Ethnicity in the Victorian ALP." *People and Place* 8, no. 1 (2000): 28-38.

ALP. "2010 ALP National Review Report." news release, 2010.

———. "National Platform 2015." 2015.

———. "Labor National Platform A Fair Go For Australia." ALP, 2018.

———. "ALP National Platform Consultation Draft." April 2018.

Anisa, Khan. "Sydney mother of three opens up about her choice to wear the niqab and life as a Muslim Australian." By Monique. Schaffer and Jeanavive McGregor. *7.30* (21 October 2014).

Arndt, Bettina. *The Sydney Morning Herald*, 21 April 1998.

Ayers, Tim. "5 Reasons Why Direct Action Isn't Good Enough." 2014.

Baldwin, Peter. "Regressive Left puts bigotry and militant Islam on a pedestal." *The Australian*, 17 September 2016.

Betts, Katharine. *The Great Divide: Immigration Politics in Australia*. Sydney, NSW: Duffy and Snellgrove, 1999.

———. "Immigration and public opinion: understanding the shift." *People and Place* 10, no. 4 (2002): 24-37.

Betts, Katherine, and Bob Birrell. "Australian voters' views' on immigration policy." The Australian Population Research Institute, 2017.

Birrell, Bob, and Ernest Healy. "Immigration and the Housing Affordability Crisis in Sydney and Melbourne ". *The Australian Population Research Institute* (July 2018).

Birrell, Bob, Ernest Healy, and Lyle Allan. "Labor's Shrinking Constituency." *People and Place* 13, no. 2 (2005): 50-67.

Birrell, Bob, and Byong-Soo Seol. "Sydney's Ethnic Underclass." *People and Place* 6, no. 3 (1998): 16-29.

Bita, Natasha. "Mums: You are a waste stuck at home." *The Daily Telegraph*, 10 March 2017.

Bolleyer, Nicole, and Anika Gauja. "The Limits of Regulation: Indirect Party Access to State Resources in Australia and the United Kingdom." *Governance: An International Journal of Policy, Administration and Insititutions* 28, no. 3 (2015).

Bongiorno, Frank. "The end of the affair?: Unions, citizens and the future of the ALP." *Australian Review of Public Affairs* (2002).

Botterill, Linda, and Alan Fenna. "Political parties and the party system." In *Government and Politcs in Australia*, edited by Alan. Fenna, Jane. Robbins and John. Summers. Frenchs Forest: Pearson, 2014.

Bowen, Chris. "The genius of Australian multiculturalism." In *The Sydney Institute*, 2011.

———. *Hearts & Minds: A Blueprint for Modern Labor*. Carlton, Vic.: Melbourne Univesity Press, 2013.

Bracks, Steve, John Faulkner, and Bob Carr. "2010 National Review: Report to the ALP National Executive." Australian Labor Party, 2010.

Bramble, Tom, and Rick Kuhn. "Continuity or Discontinuity in the Recent History of the Australian Labor Party?". *Australian Journal of Political Science* 44, no. 2 (2009): 281-94.

Bramston, Troy. "ALP told to listen to party elders in 2010 Labor national review report." *The Australian*, 24 February 2011.

———. *Looking for the Light on the Hill: Modern Labor's Challenges*. Carlton North, Vic.: Scribe, 2011.

———. "Powerbrokers give elders the brush." *The Australian*, 6 December 2011.

————. "Defeat sparks call for ALP branch overhaul." *The Australian*, 12 April 2014.

————. "ALP Conference 2015: unions still rule OK, despite minor reforms." *The Australian*, 27 July 2015.

Burgmann, Verity, and Andrew Milner. "Intellectuals and the New Social Movements." In *Class and Class conflict in Australia*, edited by Rick. Kuhn and Tom. O'Lincoln. Melbourne, Vic.: Longman, 1996.

Burnley, Ian, Peter Murphy, and Robert Fagan. *Immigration and Australian Capital Cities*. Leichhardt, NSW: Federation Press, 1997.

Button, John. "Beyond Belief: What Future for Labor?". *Quartely Essay* no. 6 (2002): 1-79.

Caldwell, Anna, and Sharri Markson. "Sheer Foley." *The Daily Telegraph*, 25 May 2018.

Calhoun, Craig. *Social Theory and the Politics of Identity*. Blackwell, 1994.

Carr, Kim. *A Letter to Generation Next: Why Labor*. Carlton, Vic.: Melbourne University Press, 2013.

Carswell, Andrew, and Ian Walker. "Sydney's Muslim community rallies in Lakemba in response to terror attacks that rocked Paris." *The Daily Telegraph*, 23 January 2015.

Cavalier, Rodney. "The Australian Labor Party at Branch Level: Guildford, Hunters Hill and Panania Branches in the 1950s.". In *A Century of Social Change: Labor History Essays Volume Four*, edited by Australian Labor Party, 1992.

————. "There is no working class." *Southern Highlands Branch Newsletter*, 1999.

————. "Labor in Crisis." By James. Carleton. *Radio National* (2006).

————. *The Australian*, 13 October 2010.

————. *Power Crisis: The Self-destruction of a State Labor Party*. Port Melbourne, Vic.: Cambridge University Press, 2010.

————. "Submission ot the Panel of Experts - Political Donations." 2014.

Cavalier, Rodney, Lindsay Tanner, Joe de Bruyn, and Chris Christodoulou. "Simon Says: Federal Labor's crisis of confidence and how Simon Crean is dealing with it" By Liz Jackson. *Four Corners* (2002).

Chifley, Ben. "These things are really worth fighting for." In *Annual Conference of the NSW Branch*, 1948.

Coghlan, Jo, and Scott Denton. "The irony of the ACTU's defence of the ALP." On Line Opinion, 2012.

———. "Reviewing Labor's Internal Reviews 1966-2010: 'Looking forward, looking backwards'." *Melbourne Journal of Politics* 35 (2012): 19-38.

Cohen, Barry. *The Australian*, 24 October 1996.

Crean, Simon. "ALP convenes to hear Hawke-Wran-Wran recommendations." By Alexandra. Kirk. *The World Today* (9 August 2002).

———. "ALP must modernise and be more inclusive." Paper presented at the ALP National Left Conference, 2002.

Crean, Simon, Bob Hawke, Neville Wran, and Joan Kirner. "Crean to fight for Hawke-Wran proposals." By Louise. Yaxley. *PM* (9 August 2002).

Creighton, Adam. "Labor's identity politics - the left's blight on the hill." *The Australian*, 30 April 2018.

Crisp, L. F. "The Labor Party: Then and Now." In *Labor Essays 1982: Socialist Principles and Parliamentary Government*, edited by Gareth. Evans and John. Reeves, 65-81. Richmon, Vic.: Drummond Publishing, 1982.

Cross, William, and Anika Gauja. "Evolving membership strategies in Australian political parties." *Australian Journal of Political Science* 49, no. 4 (2014): 611-25.

Crowe, David. "Newspoll: Coalition on slide as voters turn to Pauline Hanson." *The Australian*, 27 February 2017.Cumming, Fia, and Andrew West. "ALP: It's time for reform." *Sydney Morning Herald*, 6 October 2002.

Daley, Janet. "Corbyn's win a bad omen for a once-vital progressive party." *National Post*, 14 September 2015.

Davidson, Kenneth. "Flimsy whimsy of Hawke and Wran won't save Labor."

The Age, 12 August 2002.

Deverall, Kate, Rebecca Huntley, Penny Sharpe, and Jo Tilly, eds. *Party Girls: Labor Women Now*. Annandale, NSW: Pluto Press, 2000.

Dunn, Kevin M, Natascha Klocker, and Tanya Salabay. "Contemporary racism and Islamaphobia in Australia: Racializing religion." *Ethnicities* 7, no. 4 (2007): 564-89.

Dyrenfurth, Nick. "It's time Labor went back to the workers." *The Weekend Australian*, 22-23 October 2011.

———. "Labor's damaged Right faction must renew." *The Saturday Paper*, 18 April 2015 2015.

Easson, Michael. "The Right approach for a tired organisation." *The Weekend Australian*, 8-9 December 2012.

Encel, Sol. "Labor and the Future: Where to now?". *Evatt Journal* 5, no. 2 (2005). Essential Media Communications. "Statement about immigration." *Essential Report* (2016). Published electronically 18 May 2016.

Essential Research. "The Essential Media Report,." 2 August 2016.Ethnic Communities' Council of Victoria. "Submission to the Discussion Paper, Australian Citizenship: Much more than a ceremony." 2006.

Faulkner, John. "Cultural reform essential for Labor." *The Australian*, 10 June 2011.

———. "Public Pessism, Political Complacency, Restoring Trust, Reforming Labor." In *The Light on the Hill Society*, 2014.

Fitzgerald, Stephen. "Immigration - A commitment to Australia." Canberra: Australian Government Publishing Service, 1989.

Frank, Thomas. *Listen Liberal or Whatever Happened To The Party Of The People*. Melbourne: Scribe, 2016.

Franklin, Matthew, and Milanda Rout. "ALP Review authors urge no more secrets." *The Australian*, 6 December 2011.

Freudenberg, Graham. *A Certain Grandeur: Gough Whitlam's Life in Politics*. South

Melbourne, Vic.: Sun Books, 1978.

Gauja, Anika. *Party reform: the causes, challenges, and consequences of organizational change* Oxford University Press, 2016.

Gerth, H. H., and C. Wright Mills, eds. *From Max Weber: Essays in Sociology.* New York: Oxford Univesity Press, 1946.

Gleeson, Hayley, and Julia Baird. "'I'm not his property': Abused Muslim women denied right to divorce." (2018). Published electronically 18 April 2018.

Glezer, Helen, and Ilene Wolcott. "Work and family values, preferences and practice." 4 (September 1997).

Glover, Barney. "Challenging cultural and social divides." *The Daily Telegraph*, 21 May 2015.

Goot, Murray. "Party Convergence Reconsidered." *Australian Journal of Political Science* 39, no. 1 (2004): 49-75.

Gray, Darren, and Sophie Douez. "Unions back the thrust of Hawke, Wran report." *The Age*, 10 August 2002.

Hartcher, Peter. "Beholden to the cargo cult: Australia's political class letting us down." *Sydney Morning Herald*, 15 December 2017.

Hasham, Nicole. "NSW election: Muslim group turns on Labor leader Luke Foley in Auburn." *The Sydney Morning Herald*, 26 March 2015.

Haslam, Nick. "Bigots are just sick at heart." *The Australian*, 17 December 2008.

Hassan, Riaz, and Bill Martin. "Islamophobia, social distance and fear of terrorism in Australia: A Preliminary Report." University of South Australia, 2015.

Hawke, Bob, and Neville Wran. "National Committee of Review." 2002.

Hayden, Bill. *Sydney Morning Herald*, 27 January 1981.

Hayden, Bill, and Bob Hawke. "National Committee of Inquiry: Report and Recommendations to the National Executive." Australian Labor Party, 1979.

Hayden, Bill., and Bob. Hawke. "National Committee of Inquiry." Australian Labor Party, 1979.

Healy, Ernest, and Bob Birrell. "Metropolis divided: The political dynamics of spatial inequality and migrant settlement in Sydney." *People and Place* 11, no. 2 (2003): 16-29.

Hetherington, David. "What Price the Gap? Education and Inequality in Australia." Public Education Foundation, 2018.

Hirst, John. "National Pride and Multiculturalism." *People and Place* 2, no. 3 (1994): 1-6.Howard, John. *Lazarus Rising: A Personal and Political Autobiography.* Pymble, NSW: HarperCollins, 2010.

Hunter, Fergus. "Half of Australia's 12,000 Syrian and Iraqi refugees to be settled by just one Sydney council." *Sydney Morning Herald,* 16 January 2017.

Hurford, Chris. "Chris Hurford: Silver lining to Hilali." *The Australian,* 2 November 2006.Iner, Derya (ed.). "Islamophobia in Australia." Charles Sturt University, 2017.

Johns, Gary. "Labor risks taking its democracy too far." *The Australian,* 8 December 2011.

Joint Standing Committee on Migration. "Inquiry into Migration and Multiculturalism in Australia." The Parliament of the Commonwealth of Australia, 2013.

Jones, Owen. *Chavs: The Demonisation of the Working Class.* London, UK: Verso, 2012.

Jupp, James, ed. *The Australian People: An Encyclopaedia of the Nation, Its Peoples and their Origin.* Cambridge, UK: Cambridge University Press, 2001.

Karp, Paul. "Pauline Hanson's One Nation triples support since election: Newspoll." *The Guardian,* 17 October 2016.

Katz, Richard S, and Peter Mair. "Changing Models of Party Organization and Party Democracy: The Emergence of the Cartel Party." *Party Politics* 1, no. 1 (1995): 5-28.

Kelly, Paul. "Bill's fixes fine for opposition, but not government." *The Australian,*

19 December 2018.

―――. *The End of Certainty: Power, Politics and Business in Australia*. St. Leonards, NSW: Allen & Unwin, 1994

.―――. "Race, gender: the risk of identity politics." *The Australian*, 6 August 2016.

Knott, Mathew, and Adam. Gatrell. "The six big issues to be debated at Labor's national conference." *Sydney Morning Herald*, 24 July 2015.

Knott, Matthew., and Adam. Gartrell. "The six big issues to be debated at Labor's national conference." *Sydney Morning Herald*, 24 July 2015.

Le Messurier, Danielle. "Remark Raises Foley Hell." *The Daily Telegraph*, 25 May 2018.

Lehmann, Claire. "We must resist the scourge of 'identity politics'." *The Drum* (2015). Published electronically 26 June 2015.

Leigh, Andrew. "Factions and Fractions: A Case Study of Power Politics in the Australian Labor Party." *Australian Journal of Political Science* 35, no. 3 (2000): 427-48.

Lloyd, Clem. "A quest for national rules." In *The Machine: Labor confronts the future*, edited by John. Warhurst and Andrew. Parkin. St Leonards, NSW: Allen & Unwin, 2000.

Lopez, Mark. *The Origins of Multiculturalism in Australian Politics 1945-1975*. Carlton South, Vic.: Melbourne University Press, 2000.

―――. "The Politics of the Origins of Multiculturalism." *People and Place* 8, no. 1 (2000): 22-28.

Maly, Paul. "Islam critic Ayaan Hirsi Ali cancels tour." *The Australian*, 4 April 2017.

Manne, Robert. "Beware the new racism." *The Age*, 16 September 2002.

―――. "Open Season on Muslims in the Newest Phobia." *Sydney Morning Herald*, 16 September 2002.

Markus, Andrew. "Attitudes To Multiculturalism and Cultural Diversity." In

Multiculturalism and Integration: a Harmonious Relationship, edited by James. Jupp and Michael. Clyne. Canberra, ACT: ANU Press, 2011.

———. "Not prejudiced on asylum issue." *The Australian*, 27 September 2011

.———. "Mapping Social Cohesion: The Scanlon Foundation Survey 2017 ", 2017.

Markus, Andrew, and Margaret Taft. "Postwar Immigration and Assimilation: A Reconceptualisation." *Australian Historical Studies* 46, no. 2 (2015): 234-51.

Marsh, Ian. "Australia's political cartel?". In *Political Parties in Transition?*, edited by Ian. Marsh. Annandale, NSW: The Federation Press, 2006.

McMullin, Ross. *The Light on the Hill: The Australian Labor Party, 1891-1991*. Oxford: Oxford University Press Australia, 1991.

McNair, Brian. "Islam and the media - let's not fear open debate." (2015). Published electronically 20 April 2015. http://theconversation.com/islam-and-the-media-lets-not-fear-open-debate-40468.

Merritt, Chris. "Sharia law at work in Australia." *The Australian*, 20 July 2011.

Miller, Charles. "Australia's anti-Islam right in their own words. A text as data analysis of social media content." *Australian Journal of Political Science* 52, no. 383-401 (2017).

Mills, Stephen. *The Professionals: Strategy, Money and the Rise of the Political Campaigner*. Collingwood, Vic.: Black Inc., 2014.

Montoya, Daniel, and Jack Finegan. "Background Paper No 04/2014." NSW Parliamentary Research Service, 2014.

Murray, Robert. *The Split: Australian Labor in the Fifties*. Sydney, NSW: Hale & Ironmonger, 1984.

National Consultative Review Committee. "Report by the National Consultative Review Committee to the ALP National Executive." ALP, August 1996.

Nelson, Paul. "Socio-economic indexes for 2009 electoral divisions: 2006 Census." Parliamentary Library, 2010.

Newman, Gerard. "Federal Election Results 1949-1998." *Research Paper* (1999).

Published electronically 9 February 1999.

Nicholls, Sean. "Celebrated principal Jihad Dib to be parachuted in as ALP candidate despite John Robertson's democracy claim." *The Sydney Morning Herald*, 5 September 2014.

Norington, Brad, and Sid Maher. "Union boss Tony Sheldon rejects call to cut party power." *The Australian*, 9 October 2014.

Norrington, Brad. "Complex truth of "white flight" revealed in data." *The Australian*, 16 June 2018.

O'Connell, Declan. "Party Reform: Debates & Dilemmas, 1958-1991." In *A Century of Social Change Labor History Essays*, edited by Australian Labor Party. New South Wales Branch, 134-57. Leichhardt, N.S.W: Pluto Press Australia, 1992.

O'Hanlon, Seamus, and Rachel Stevens. "A Nation of Immigrants or a Nation of Immigrant Cities? The Urban Context of Australian Multiculturalism." *Australian Journal of Political Science* 63, no. 4 (2017): 556-71.

O'Neill, P. "Youth Unemployment in Western Sydney." Centre for Western Sydney, 2017.

Oakes, Laurie. "Reforms needed or Labor will die." *The Daily Telegraph*, 3 December 2011.

Osborne, Samuel. "Australian school allows male Muslim pupils to refuse handshakes with women." *Independent*, 20 February 2017.

Panebianco, Angelo. *Political Parties: Organization and Power*. Cambridge, England: Cambridge University Press, 1988.

Patty, Anna. "John Faulkner's preselection proposal faces defeat." *Illawarra Mercury*, 18 July 2014.

Piketty, Thomas. "Brahmin Left v Merchant Right: Rising Inequality & the Changing Structure of Political Conflict." World Inequality Database, 2018.

Probert, Belinda. "Gender and Choice: The Structure of Opportunity." In *Work of the Future: Global Perspectives*, edited by Paul. James, Walter. Veit and Steve. Wright. St Leonards, NSW: Allen & Unwin, 1997.

Qu, Lixia, and Ruth Weston. "A woman's place? Work hour preferences revisited: nearly a decade has elapsed since the report by Glezer and Wolcott on mothers' work hours preferences. Lixia Qu and Ruth Weston look at whether mothers' preferences changed during this time." *Family Matters*, no. 72 (2005): 72.

Ray, Robert. "Are Factions Killing the Labor Party?" In *Address to the Fabian Society*. Sydney, 2006.

Richardson, Graham. *Whatever It Takes*. Sydney, NSW: Bantam, 1994.

Richardson, Graham. "Talk at lunch, not in court, over Israel." *The Australian*, 4 March 2016.

Ridley, Matt. "Left is creating a new kind of apartheid." *The Times*, 28 November 2016.

Sawer, Marian. "A defeat for political correctness?". In *The Politics of Retribution: The 1996 Australian Federal Election*, edited by Clive Bean, 73-79. St. Leonards, NSW: Allen & Unwin, 1997.

Scanlon, Christopher. "A touch of class." *The Age*, 17 April 2004.

Schacht, Chris. "Labor Seats for Sale." *Sunday* (20 November 2002).

Scott, Andrew. *Fading loyalties: The Australian Labor Party and the Working Class*. Leichhardt, NSW: Pluto Press, 1991.

Siedentorp, Larry. *Inventing the Individual The Origins of Western Liberalism*. Penguin, 2014.

Sniderman, Paul M., and Louk. Hagendoorn. *When Ways of Life Collide: Multiculturalism and Its Discontents in the Netherlands*. Princeton, NJ: Princeton University Press, 2007.

Stone, John. "Remeber, it was Paul Keating." *The Australian Financial Review*, 15 March 1996.

Switzer, Tom. "Why Muslims make headlines." In *Islam and the Australian News Media*, edited by Halim. Rane, Jacqui. Ewart and Mohamad. Abdalla, 2010.

Thompson, Michael. *Labor without class: The gentrification of the ALP*. Annandale,

NSW: Pluto Press in association with the Lloyd Ross Forum, Labour Council of New South Wales, 1999.

Trad, Keysar. "Muslim leader's sexist sermon causes uproar." By Josie Talor. *The World Today* (26 October 2006).

Tran, Mark. "Australian Muslim leader compares uncovered women to exposed meat " *The Guardian*, 26 October 2006.

Urban, Rebecca. "Punchbowl School 'resisted ' Islam program." *The Australian*, 6 March 2017.

———. "Troubled Punchbowl Boys High School leadership team dumped." *The Australian*, 3 March 2017.

van Onselen, Peter. "Reform-averse politicians are letting down the nation." *The Australian*, 10 December 2016.

Ward, Ian. "Cartel parties and election campaigns in Australia." In *Political Parties in Transition*, edited by Ian. Marsh. Leichhardt, NSW: The Federation Press, 2006.

Whitington, Don. *The Witless Men.* Melbourne: Sun Books, 1975.

Whitlam, Gough. "Address to the ALP Federal Conference." 4 August 1965.

Wyndham, Cyril. "Australian Labor Party Reorganisation: Recommendations of the General Secretary ", 1964.

Zubrycki, Jerzy. *The Australian*, 15 October 1996.

Zweig, Michael. *The Working Class Majority: America's Best Kept Secret.* Ithaca, N.Y: IRL Press, 2001.

The Triumph of Identity Politics